MAKE
HOW
MATTER

Key Conversations for Leaders
to Build Alignment and Accelerate Growth

JULIE WILLIAMSON, PhD

FC

FAST
COMPANY
Press

Fast Company Press
New York, New York
www.fastcompanypress.com

This work is being published under the Fast Company Press imprint by an exclusive arrangement with Fast Company. Fast Company and the Fast Company logo are registered trademarks of Mansueto Ventures, LLC. The Fast Company Press logo is a wholly owned trademark of Mansueto Ventures, LLC.

Distributed by River Grove Books

Design and composition by Greenleaf Book Group and Sheila Parr
Cover design by Greenleaf Book Group and Sheila Parr
Cover image used under license from Adobe Stock: 3308630672/martialred

Publisher's Cataloging-in-Publication data is available.

Print ISBN: 978-1-63908-154-7

eBook ISBN: 978-1-63908-155-4

First Edition

For all the leaders who know work is better, faster, and way more fun when you do it together as a team . . .

I see you. I hear you. I've been you. And I wrote this book for you.

Contents

Alignment Resources

For interactive versions of the worksheets and additional resources to support you, please visit us at www.makehowmatter.com/worksheets.

The Karrikins Behavior Model

New Ways of Working

Implementation

Throughout the book you will see this conversation icon, often accompanied by a worksheet. Take note of these key conversations to have with your colleagues. They will help spark an understanding of how to lead and work together toward shared goals.

The most aspirational WHY and the most ambitious WHAT will fail without an aligned *HOW*.

Let's Get Started

If everyone is moving forward together, then success takes care of itself.

—Henry Ford, founder, Ford Motor Company

STOP WHATEVER YOU ARE DOING right now. Wait, no, that's a bad idea, since what you are doing is reading this book. Keep reading. While you are reading, envision your team members. Who are they? What are they good at? Where do they struggle? Is your team comprised of people who report to you? Are they contained to your area of expertise or work unit? Or did you describe a team that crosses your business—a team of interdependent peers who may not have a common reporting structure?

I suspect you envisioned some version of a vertical team structure—most people do. Yet the difference between success and failure in business today lies in the strength of horizontal teams—connected leaders across the organization making decisions and setting priorities based on the whole business, not just their part of it. They know how to lead together to create successes beyond any one person or area because they've done the work to *make HOW matter.*

There are plenty of books in the world about business, management, leadership, and teaming. I have personally been inspired by many of them. They have influenced my career, my thinking, and my approach to my work. One might suggest there's plenty out there, so why write this book? What makes this content special, different, or meaningful in the world? Why does *HOW* we lead together matter?

Have you ever sat in a meeting and thought, *Not this conversation again* or *Didn't we make this decision a month ago* or *Here those two go again down that rabbit hole . . . Wake me up when we are back to something interesting*? Have you ever seen a status report where every person or department is reporting "green," but you know full well the overall program or business is in "red"? Have you heard comments like "We need to be more innovative" or "We should be more collaborative" or "If only we'd prioritize better" and just shrugged because you know nothing will ever really change? How about this one: "Here's our transformative new strategy that is going to be the focus for this year," but you know business as usual will take over within a week? These moments come from a lack of understanding *HOW* leaders lead together to deliver exceptional outcomes.

When David Guest first started writing in the early 1990s about T-shaped leadership and horizontal leaders, he opened a new way of thinking about the importance of leading across the organization—of being a part of something more than your vertical discipline. The trend he tapped into more than thirty years ago is even more true today in businesses that are increasingly intertwined across geographies, products, go-to-market strategies, and more. And yet we continue to see people define success based on delivering what's right in front of them rather than connecting across the business to drive organizational strategies, priorities, and goals.

Business today requires new ways of leading and working together as a team toward shared goals. And that's a very, very difficult thing to do.

Despite all the agreement that people need to be able to work across their organizations, people still tend to be appointed to leadership roles because they are exceptional at technical functions—sales, engineering, design, finance, whatever. They know WHAT they do extremely well, and they deliver. Their role as a leader is in part validation of their technical expertise, and success equates to continuing to excel at delivering what they and their teams do.

Many businesses today are highly interconnected, with massive dependencies—they are, by design, complex and variable systems that work to maintain stasis in order to produce reliable results. Individual leaders contribute to this consistency by being exceptional at what they do and staying out of other people's lanes. As a result, it isn't unusual to find that leaders across geographies have all invested individually in the same financial systems to manage their territories independently, or that product leaders have spent time and money on similar innovative solutions, sometimes with the same vendor, without communicating with one another about what they are doing. This level of leader independence creates problems in many modern organizations. Not only does it fuel operational redundancies and market challenges, but it also confuses colleagues and customers and suboptimizes investments. At the same time, highly interdependent systems don't respond well to challenges; they can be bloated by bureaucracy, and they are notoriously unadaptable. Finding the right balance between autonomous leaders who run their own shops and centralized businesses that can get crushed under their own weight is a constant challenge. It can be solved by figuring out *HOW* to lead together across the enterprise so leaders have enough connective fiber to take advantage of opportunities and mitigate risks while also being able to respond quickly in their areas.

The tough reality is that the world moves too fast for a business to be slow to transform. The business school case studies of companies like Kodak and Blockbuster are certainly history lessons no one wants to repeat. Accelerating systemic transformation to an aligned organization starts at the very top, with leaders dialing into their own interconnectedness with their peers and finding ways to take advantage of and contribute to the whole business rather than working in isolation. This means senior leaders must be good not just at WHAT they do in their areas and WHY they do it but also at knowing *HOW* they do it with their teams, peers, partners, and customers. Spending time on *HOW* to lead together builds adaptability and responsiveness in individual leaders and the business without over-indexing to centralization. It creates a ripple effect of connectedness throughout a company.

As we go through this book together, we're going to explore what it looks like to spend time talking with colleagues about *HOW* to lead together. I'll give you tools, worksheets, and ideas for sparking the right conversations to shift the balance in your team from a group of great individual performers to a high-performing, cohesive team.

Too often in times of transformation, leaders focus on changing what other people do while neglecting to take on the harder work of changing how they lead. That creates a situation where leaders are doing the same things they've always done while expecting people on their teams to do things differently, which gets messy fast. As you go through this content, my hope is that you'll be inspired to pick up a pen or put your hands on a keyboard and have a go at the work of *making HOW matter*, and then engage your colleagues in the conversations as well. That's what sparks your own transformation in how you lead together.

Change *HOW* you lead before expecting others to change WHAT they do.

I am endlessly fascinated by business and all that comes with it, including the challenge of getting lots of people to move together in the same direction. At my company, Karrikins Group, my colleagues and I thrive on the challenge of helping teams come together around shared goals and objectives. It is what we do best, and this book will give you a behind-the-scenes peek at the methodologies, approaches, and thinking that inform our work with clients. It is driven by deep business acumen, decades of experience with many different types of businesses, and a social science lens that taps into how people connect and work together. This intersection brings a unique approach and theory to the work we do, and it has a proven track record of success with companies of all shapes and sizes in various industries.

I wrote this book because I believe deeply in the power of leaders and leadership teams to impact their companies, colleagues, customers, and communities for the better. In my work with my colleagues at Karrikins Group, I've engaged with hundreds of leaders and dozens of companies and seen the impact it has firsthand. But that power can only be developed if leaders like you take on the work of *making HOW matter.*

This book is full of resources to help you understand what that means and how to do it with your team.

Making It Happen

I'm not going to try to convince you that this work is easy, because it isn't. It can feel confronting and it will challenge you to engage your colleagues in different and sometimes uncomfortable ways. But if you lean into it with your colleagues, the results will be remarkable. Whether you are a CEO trying to align your executives, a new team leader leading people who used to be peers, or running a cross-organizational program that requires cooperation from various departments, this work will make all the difference in your role as a leader. It will help you accelerate results for yourself, your team, and the company. You will learn new concepts and tools for working better with your colleagues, customers, and business partners. You'll find great ideas for how to connect more deeply with any group you participate with, be it family, friends, colleagues, or your secret garage band. Taking the time to build a shared understanding of *HOW* to lead and work together can happen anywhere that two or more people are trying to deliver something as a team.

Throughout this book, you will find worksheets and tools you can use on the spot or download for use with your team. These are also located online at www.makehowmatter.com/worksheets, together with videos and other resources that will help you in pursuit of *making HOW matter*. I encourage you to think about a specific scenario within your team or organization as you go through the chapters and explore the steps to defining *HOW* you lead together to solve that scenario. Afterward, work through the book's resources with your colleagues, cocreating how you work differently as a team. This work is best done in conversation with others, so the more you leverage the tools and resources to engage with your colleagues, the better!

When you do the work to *make HOW matter*, you secure business outcomes that simply aren't possible with a misaligned team. The work is hard, but it is also rewarding, and I'm excited that you are ready to start shifting into a whole new way of leading successfully together. Let's get going!

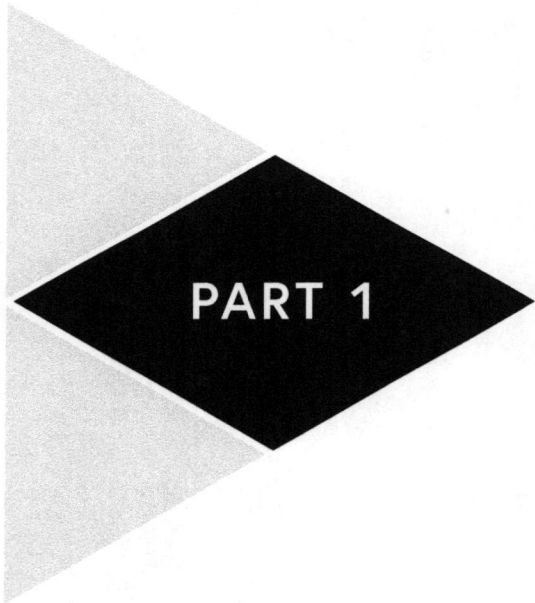

PART 1

Understanding the Problem

To go fast, go alone.
To go far, go together.
To go far fast, get aligned.

1

The Failure Gap: Where Good Ideas Go to Die

We didn't do anything wrong, but somehow, we lost.

—Stephen Elop, CEO of Nokia from 2010 to 2014

ANYONE WHO HAS EVER MADE a New Year's resolution knows the difference between *agreement* and *alignment*. Most would agree that resolutions are good, healthy, or positive—very few people commit to smoking more cigarettes or spending more time watching TV. But our good intentions fail to result in action when we don't align our decisions and behaviors to live the life we envision with our resolutions. That's the Failure Gap—the space between agreeing that something is a good idea and taking action to make it happen.

The same happens in the workplace. It is easy to *agree* that a new strategy is a good idea or transformation is necessary. It is easy to *agree* that more collaboration, better prioritization, or stronger innovation would be a good thing. It is easy to *agree* on a lot of things. It is much harder to *align* as leaders and start to work differently together. The data is consistent year after year—almost 80 percent of New Year's resolutions don't make it past the first few weeks of the year, and I'd speculate that as many transformation efforts in business fail to provide the return on investment (ROI) that was promised.

The Space Between Agreement and Alignment

Executives are charged with meeting a dizzying array of conflicting expectations, including delivering on quarterly financials, investing in long-term growth, and providing reassurance to jittery customers and markets while also being innovative, disrupting the status quo, introducing new products, reliably delivering on legacy products, maintaining employee focus and productivity, and managing rapidly shifting distribution models (just to name a few). It sounds exhausting, and for many leaders, it's almost impossible to juggle it all well. When that's the case (and I'd argue it is the case for many organizations today, whether they realize it or not), it's easy to fall into the Failure Gap—the space between agreement and alignment—when it comes to cross-organizational priorities like transformation. This is where good intentions get lost in the busyness of business as usual.

At a senior level, the Failure Gap shows up when executive teams come to agreement on priorities, strategies, opportunities to pursue, or transformational changes that are needed without doing the hard work of aligning on *HOW* to lead it together. And so, leaders all agree that changes must happen, but nothing changes because leaders very quickly revert back to business as usual. The same decisions, investments, and priorities are maintained across the organization. Deeper in the organization, the Failure Gap opens up when teams agree to support efforts or take on more work without having clarity on what needs to stop to make the capacity available. Have you ever been in that situation? I often talk to clients who say things like "We never say no to things; we just keep adding to the list" or "Everything is a priority, so nothing gets done well" or the one that really breaks my heart, "We keep getting signed up for things when we can't do what we're already committed to, and it feels hopeless."

To help you recognize the Failure Gap, check out the following differences between agreement and alignment:

AGREEMENT happens when leaders like an idea or share a sense of desire for a defined future state.	ALIGNMENT happens when leaders redirect time, energy, and resources to deliver the agreed-to future state.
Generally liking an idea	Creating a shared understanding of the idea and what it will take
Continuing with the status quo behavior	Actively working to change behavior to support the future state
Supporting an idea but not changing personal or team priorities or resource allocations	Reallocating personal and team resources and shifting priorities to make it happen
Continuing to focus on and deliver on historically appropriate goals	Building new success measures and working toward them
Voicing support for WHAT needs to be done and WHY	Doing the work to define HOW to work together to deliver

Does the agreement column sound frustratingly familiar? When you aim to transform an organization or a team, staying stuck in agreement means the desired outcome gets sucked into the Failure Gap.

The space between agreement and alignment is stark. Agreement is a nice-to-have—it doesn't require much more than good intentions and a smile. Alignment is an imperative—it requires action and is where the hard work happens. That's why I believe that aligning horizontally to new ways of leading together is nonnegotiable if a leadership team is going to succeed at transforming a company, delivering on strategic ambitions, and moving confidently toward the future. And if you are a team leader trying to get your team members working together, especially in a matrix structure or with colleagues who don't report directly to you, alignment to plans, priorities, and goals is crucial.

Moving a team across the Failure Gap from agreement to alignment is a powerful leadership skill. It helps to:

» Reduce circular conversations

» Infuse velocity into decision-making

» Accelerate momentum for transformation

» Create urgency and action on strategy

» Make it visible when priorities aren't being resourced

» Move from ideas to execution, especially on strategic goals

» Create a sense of connection across the team with pride in shared accomplishments

When leaders are stuck in agreement, heads are nodding, but nothing else is moving. Getting aligned means putting new ways of leading and working into action, often making difficult choices to drive productive outcomes. When leaders do the work to align, they see the impact immediately:

» Resources are reallocated to make sure people have what they need to move priorities forward.

» Activities and investments are deprioritized or discontinued to create the capacity to move toward the future.

» Legacy ways of leading and working start to shift in meaningful ways.

» Deeply embedded leadership habits are changed.

» Legacy distribution and supply chains are disrupted.

» Transformation efforts start to come to life internally and externally.

Remember, the Failure Gap is the space between agreement and alignment. It is the gap between agreeing that something sounds good and changing decisions and behaviors to do it. Alignment means figuring out how you are going to take action—the commitments you need to make and the courage you need to show when it is hard to do what you agree you should do.

> **Alignment is knowing _HOW_ to lead differently together to deliver on your most ambitious goals.**

CASE STUDY

The Failure Gap in Action

When a team or company is struggling to move from agreement to alignment, change is impossible. So, how do you avoid or get out of the Failure Gap? Do the work to get aligned as a team. Let's start with an example that probably sounds familiar to a lot of people.

I wish I could source the quote "We need to stop working in silos and start collaborating." I can't, because it is actually a quote from virtually every team I've ever worked with—more than I can count. There is one team leader I'll never forget. I'll call her Sara here. Sara was a highly successful leader, who had hundreds of global resources reporting to her. She and her seven peer leaders worked for a global tech company, and their teams

> **We need to stop working in silos and start collaborating.**

supported operations for customers in every corner of the world. Between them, they were responsible for negotiating priorities and allocating resources to keep customers purchasing the technology their company made.

Let's call this group of peer leaders Tech Team 1 (TT1). Each member of TT1 was fantastic at their job. They knew WHAT they were doing and WHY they were doing it. Individually, they were highly competent. They all worked their little piece of the empire with little to no connection to one another.

While these leaders were reasonably successful in their individual areas, the group was falling behind on goals for new sales, renewals, and customer satisfaction. Their global customers were getting confused by mixed messages from across the company, and the operations teams supporting these customers were equally frustrated. As leaders, they were missing opportunities to learn, adapt, and accelerate improvement throughout the global footprint.

Despite their individual abilities to deliver, the TT1 leaders fell into the Failure Gap around collaboration, and it was impacting their business results.

Sara's team of leaders kept saying things like "We really should collaborate more." But when it came to putting those ways of working into action . . . well, just imagine one of those awkward family dinners where your crazy uncle just said something really inappropriate and everyone looks around trying not to engage, and you'll get the picture. When asked for an example of collaboration, they'd shuffle their feet, look off into the distance, and come up with some farfetched time they talked with another team member about something—which, by the way, is not collaboration.

They had big strategic goals that required collaborative work across their teams. They also had endlessly detailed execution plans for each of their areas. In other words, they knew WHAT they needed to do. They understood the company mission, vision, and values and WHY these were important. They just didn't know *HOW* to do it together.

They did quarterly business reviews (QBRs) that sent everyone into a mad scramble the last two weeks of the quarter. If you do the math, that's eight weeks out of the year—two months of time and energy—sidelined by preparing individual reports. Theoretically, QBRs were the perfect place to collaborate and connect the dots across the business, but the excruciating PowerPoint presentations were designed to overwhelm any dialogue with data to prevent questions. No one wanted to hear a question they couldn't answer, and everyone worked to dial down possible left-field ideas. The goal of each leader was to stand up, present their report, and sit down as quickly as possible.

When it came to QBRs, no one was happy. Even the senior executives Sara reported to could see the team members were missing opportunities to process and discuss the information. Deeper in the organization, the boots-on-the-ground people working with customers knew they were falling behind from a technology and product perspective, and they wondered if the leadership team had any idea of what was happening. Customers were frustrated with having to interact with disconnected parts of the business to get the multiple products they were purchasing from the same company to work together.

And yet, the team leaders were stuck in a cycle of nonstop, heads-down, siloed work to meet their quarterly numbers and get their presentations organized so they didn't risk reputational damage or business challenges, or cause the leaders above them to question their capabilities. They had gone through endless reorganization efforts to spur collaboration, and senior management had mucked around with the compensation plan more than once. They had put objectives and key results (OKRs) and management by objectives (MBOs) in place to create incentives to collaborate more, but most people had figured out how to manipulate the system to check boxes without doing anything differently. The team knew WHAT to do: collaborate! And they knew WHY they needed to do it: to get better results for customers and colleagues. And yet . . . they struggled.

Sara and her colleagues hadn't tackled personal mindsets and the group dynamics that were getting in the way of working together. They weren't being transparent about the trade-offs they needed to make to collaborate with one another. They avoided the conversation of *HOW* to lead differently together to create the outcomes they wanted. Without bringing clarity and connection to *HOW* they needed to orient toward collaborating, they couldn't commit to new actions or change. They were stuck in the Failure Gap—in agreement but not taking concrete action.

Recognizing the Failure Gap

Why is understanding the Failure Gap important? Because leaders who are busy treading water fail to see new opportunities and threats flooding the market. In fact, maintaining the status quo and being "just fine" provides a false sense of security. Keep in mind that companies who were "doing fine" until they weren't include Kodak, Blockbuster, Sony Music, and Nokia Mobile . . . not the best company to keep!

Leaders like the members of TT1 are often very busy being good at what they do in their vertical areas of the business. They have scorecards to work toward and goals to meet. Investing time and energy to connect across the business doesn't feel important or urgent, especially for leaders who are already working long, stressful hours in their own areas in order to meet their objectives.

This is one of the reasons why collaboration is a great example of misalignment. While most people agree that collaboration is a good idea, they don't do the work to figure out how to do it together because it means making some uncomfortable beliefs visible. Often, in my experience, people create or face the following obstacles related to aligning their behaviors to collaborate more with their colleagues:

» **Individual mindsets** stop people from changing how they work to incorporate collaboration. These mindsets might sound like *Collaboration takes too long, I don't want to involve other people who don't really understand the problem*, or *I want to maintain control over the decisions*. It's easy to skip collaboration when making quarterly numbers and drama-free QBRs are priorities.

» **Group dynamics** like the ideas of *staying in my lane, respecting their authority*, or *not getting into other people's business* are commonly held norms that prevent collaboration from happening. During opportunities to connect like QBRs, questions are avoided. *Get through and get on* is often the underlying sentiment, born out of good intentions—putting a colleague on blast in front of senior management would not be cool.

» **Organizational factors** get in the way too. Metrics that reward speed over systematic solutions, recognition programs that reward firefighters and heroes, and compensation systems that make shared rewards difficult to manage are some of the organizational factors that can get in the way of working together. Even reporting structures often keep everyone in their own geographic areas.

You might think collaboration efforts fail due to a lack of metrics, ineffective communication, or inadequate training. It's also easy to blame others or cite a capacity issue for the lack of alignment. However, less obvious but highly influential human dynamics are often the more likely culprit. There's no doubt it is hard to address these often-invisible influencers of behaviors—it is a lot easier to build a process diagram than to get someone to articulate a deeply held belief! We're going to get into ways to open up these types of conversations as we go forward through this book and discover ways to move from agreement to alignment by changing the discussions we are having with colleagues.

For TT1, the ever-widening Failure Gap around collaboration was fueled by individual mindsets, group dynamics, and organizational factors that prevented change from happening. I'm willing to bet you've felt this sense of being stuck in an unproductive way of working with colleagues. Everyone agrees it should be different somehow, but it's business as usual, and inertia is too strong to break away from. It's so frustrating, isn't it?

In the TT1 example, Sara and her team knew they were in the Failure Gap, and they knew the risks it introduced. They just didn't know how to be different as a team. They were all very, very busy, and spending time as a team felt like a luxury they couldn't afford. In fairness, Sara's team had tried plenty of team-building trends, including style profiles for their personalities, communication, and work preferences. They had been on field trips to highly collaborative environments. They'd done collaboration workshops, and they'd all pushed their vertical team members to collaborate more. Unfortunately, defining *HOW* to lead and work together isn't a team-building exercise. TT1 needed to do the hard work of articulating and wrestling with how they each viewed collaboration and how they, as leaders, needed to change their own belief structures to collaborate more with one another.

Rather than agreeing to more nice words on a page (*respectful! honest! curious! collaborative!*), they needed to dig deeper together and give voice to their individual mindsets and the group dynamics that were getting in the way of collaboration. These are tough topics to work through, and they don't emerge in a single catalytic discussion or team-building session. And the work can't be outsourced to other people—the leaders themselves had to commit the time and energy to figure it out together.

Leaders can't delegate alignment work.

▶ Self-Assessment—Seven Signs of Misalignment

For Sara and TT1, they were misaligned to the agreement to "collaborate more." We are going to come back to them shortly. Right now, though, I'd like for you to think about where you see misalignment on your team or in your organization. It might be something different—a big strategic goal, a market shift, a product enhancement, wanting to be more innovative, or better prioritization. Take a minute and consider where you might be in the Failure Gap.

One way to understand if there might be a challenge is to self-assess. We see seven signs of misalignment that indicate an issue. Have a look through these, and use the worksheet to have a conversation with your team about how they would self-assess how the team works together:

1. **Meeting topics are on repeat—we have the same conversations over and over.** If your meetings feel monotonous, it could mean there's a lack of clarity around and connection to how to move forward together. That keeps teams stuck in a loop, wondering why no one is doing what they said they'd do.

2. **Decision rights are unclear, and decision-making is slow.** When decision-making takes too long, it hinders progress, slows responsiveness to challenges, and leads to missed opportunities. This sluggish pace indicates a need for clearer communication, streamlined processes, and a more aligned approach to problem-solving.

3. **Discussions and decisions happen outside of meetings, not in them.** This tendency diminishes the effectiveness of scheduled meetings, where effective decision-making, brainstorming, and problem-solving should ideally take place. It breaks down communication and can lead to information gaps, and even fuel animosity between team members who feel left out.

4. **Interdependencies and broader impacts aren't well managed.** If leaders don't understand interdependencies, it can lead to missed deadlines and struggles to achieve shared goals. Not appreciating these interconnections creates a significant hurdle for the team, making it harder for everyone to work together effectively.

5. **Everyone's status is green, but we aren't keeping up.**
   This often highlights a focus on short-term measurements and
   a neglect of longer-term ambitions that require transformative
   effort. It's a high-risk indicator of misalignment because it gives
   the impression things are "fine" when they are far from it.

6. **Stated priorities aren't adequately funded or
   resourced.** This mismatch between words and actions sends
   a signal that leaders are not fully committed. When budgets
   don't align with priorities, people assume leaders aren't serious,
   and they think they should feel free to do the same with their
   discretionary energy, effort, and time.

7. **Accountability for results/outcomes is limited.**
   Accountability takes commitment and courage from a team.
   Limited accountability leads to uncertainty about who is
   driving the success or failure of team endeavors. That creates
   a risk that important goals may not be accomplished and
   opportunities will be missed.

Check out our self-assessment tool here or online at www.makehow
matter.com/worksheets to see how you would evaluate your team. Then ask
your colleagues to contribute to the thinking and see what they notice.

Take note that all seven signs are about humans connecting and working together to deliver. And they all require people's decisions and behaviors
to shift in order to improve. It sounds easy, but you don't need much more
than your own lived experience to know that it is incredibly difficult to
change how people work together.

THE **KARRIKINS**® ALIGNMENT EVALUATION TOOL™

INSTRUCTIONS: For each statement, think about whether you hear something similar within your group. Is it something you r**arely** experience, **sometimes** experience, or **typically** experience?

When you are done, take a look at what you've created and how aligned or misaligned you think your team or group might be. This is a great way to have a rich discussion with your colleagues about the impact of misalignment in how you work together to deliver.

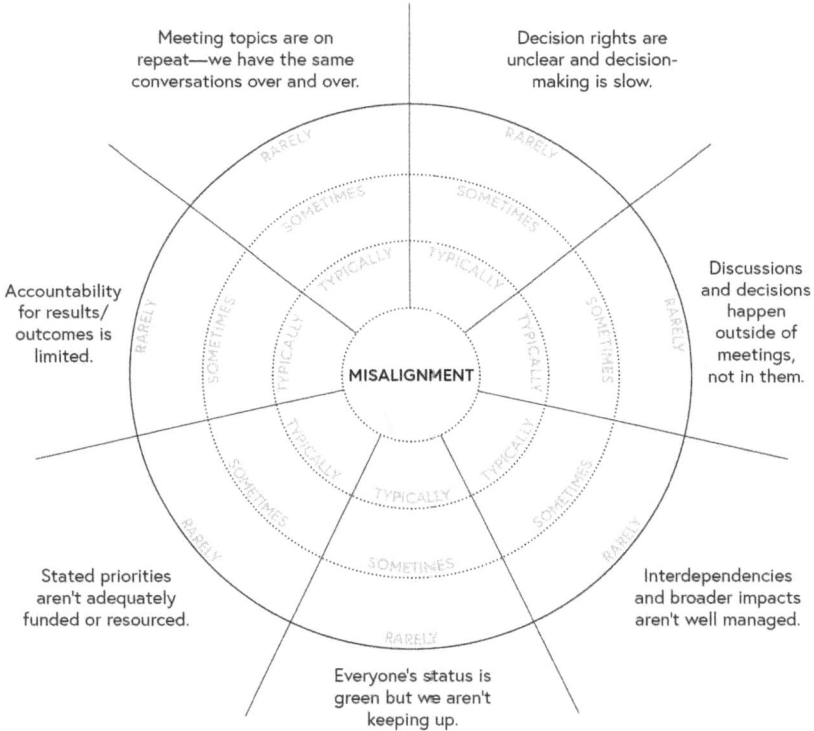

Meeting topics are on repeat—we have the same conversations over and over.

Decision rights are unclear and decision-making is slow.

Accountability for results/ outcomes is limited.

Discussions and decisions happen outside of meetings, not in them.

MISALIGNMENT

Stated priorities aren't adequately funded or resourced.

Interdependencies and broader impacts aren't well managed.

Everyone's status is green but we aren't keeping up.

Image 1.1: Seven Signs of Misalignment Worksheet

There are six big hurdles for moving through the Failure Gap that leaders must address to align and deliver together. These are some of the barriers leaders hit when they attempt to do something as a team without doing the hard work of getting aligned on how to lead together:

1. **Delegation is a dud.** Leaders sometimes try to delegate alignment work to people on their teams in the name of providing opportunity or developing the next level of leaders. It is a nice idea, but it doesn't work. It would be like delegating your bicep curls to someone else—and they develop new muscles while yours continue to atrophy.

2. **Catalytic experiences don't work.** Building new ways of working as a leadership team so you drive different strategic outcomes for your organization doesn't happen in a one-day workshop or a catalytic event. They can be a piece of the work, but alignment requires developing shared language and fluency around how to lead differently through structured conversations over time.

3. **Maintenance is a must.** Creating alignment isn't a one-and-done deal. Leaders must continuously nurture their alignment with one another. Working well together in support of shared goals is a learned experience that must be maintained with vigilant effort. The balance between independence and interdependence has to be monitored, and the work never stops. But it does get easier over time.

4. **Examples must be modeled.** It is up to leaders to model the way for others through their own behavior and by making their alignment to their peers visible to others. Good leaders show their vertical teams that they are working horizontally across the organization and are connected by emphasizing the impact their decisions have on other areas of the business.

5. **Enterprise connections must be made.** Many leaders stall out in their careers when they step up to enterprise-level

leadership and have to connect across a company with peers and people who don't report to them. Some people fail to make this transition because they don't know how to align and deliver together—they get stuck in their small part of the business. If you are in a senior leadership role, you must take on the responsibility of building connections across the company.

6. **Individuals need to take responsibility.** Alignment can't be outsourced to consultants, human resources departments, or internal communications teams. Getting support to structure and facilitate the right conversations is helpful, but leaders must own the responsibility for doing the work together and then visibly model the way for others. Think of it like organizational therapy—a good therapist helps, but at the end of the day, you do the work.

Explore for Yourself

Explore some of the things you hear a lot about in your organization. Do you see agreement but not alignment to important goals? I'm guessing it is pretty easy to recognize places where there is a lack of alignment. Most companies face similar issues. Even at Karrikins Group, it takes constant attention and effort to push past the urge to simply agree that something sounds like a good idea and hope someone else will take action—while I get on with my "very important work."

Take a few minutes to think about where there is a lot of agreement but limited action taken to drive results within your company or team. Here's a list of very common examples we hear:

» Collaboration

» Innovation

» Prioritization of programs

» Faster decision-making

- » Strategic planning

- » Improving operations

- » Improving customer experience

- » Product design

- » Go-to-market transformation

- » Focus on employees

As you think about this, consider having a conversation with your colleagues about where they are noticing agreement but not alignment. You can check out our Notice and Name worksheet on the resources page and start to catalog some of your observations. Look for where you notice your colleagues agree regarding good ideas but struggle to align and deliver results. By noticing them and giving them a name, you can kick-start the process of getting aligned in those situations. Bringing visibility and clarity to things that are in the Failure Gap is the first step in getting out of it!

Don't hesitate to grab a piece of paper, write your list here or elsewhere, or download the worksheet.

Like Sara and her team, you and your colleagues are probably great at your jobs. Perhaps you also run a global team that serves customers in every time zone. Your responsibilities run you ragged day in and day out, and there isn't a single day you wake up with nothing to do.

Could you have a serious leadership-capacity problem that is amplified because you aren't leveraging the work across your organization? Do you sit in meetings with other leaders and have respectful, surface-level conversations while avoiding the tough topics you need to deal with together? Do you and your associates duplicate efforts, chase down the same customer emergencies, and put money into systems and processes that are already working in other areas of the business? Is it common to jump on questions or requests from senior executives like they are grenades instead of

NOTICE AND NAME WORKSHEET

The Notice and Name worksheet helps shine a light on situations where agreement is there, but alignment is lacking. Look for conversations that happen over and over, habituated responses, common expressions of "should dos," and lack of inertia in your organization. They can be big or small things.

What are you noticing? Think about situations that keep coming up or things people like to say but not do.	**What would you name it?** Names can be literal, playful, or abstract—whatever works best!

Image 1.2: Notice and Name Worksheet

connecting with the leaders of other areas or divisions first, only to discover later that three of you were working on the same issue?

This last one was true for Sara's team. Another sore spot around the lack of alignment to the idea of collaborating more as a team was that it wasn't unusual for several leaders to respond to urgent requests from senior executives without knowing they were all working on the same thing. The lack of clarity and connection across the team was contributing to their capacity issue, even though they believed their focus, intensity, and quick response time was what

Companies fail to align and deliver on strategic goals while leaders are busy doing other things.

was required of them to succeed. Does any of that sound familiar?

Sara's team members were in the Failure Gap and digging themselves deeper every day. They said they wanted to work differently, but they weren't making it happen. They wanted quick and easy solutions that would get them back to their very busy day jobs as fast as possible. They hoped for a technological tool, a novel process to follow, or a quick team-building exercise to force collaboration. Could you and your team be digging the same hole because of a capacity issue?

Even a team that is insanely busy benefits from the acceleration that happens when you carve out the time to have crucially important conversations about *HOW* to lead together. We're going to walk through these conversations together, but first, you might want to check out our interactive exercise The Space Between, which you can find here: www.makehowmatter.com/worksheets. In this exercise, you and your team can explore agreement and alignment to see where your team might be stuck. In doing The Space Between exercise, it can be helpful to get together with colleagues to brainstorm your collective agreement and alignment statements. Focus on the few that would have material impact on your customers or colleagues if they were addressed. Then use the outcomes from the exercise as you go through this book to think about how the team could get better aligned.

Another way to start mining input from your colleagues is to get them to self-assess where they see the team by using the Karrikins Alignment Maturity Model. The Maturity Model helps you to have a conversation with your colleagues and figure out where you might be currently performing as a team on most things. Think about how you often work together and see if you can pinpoint the level where your team tends to operate.

KARRIKINS® ALIGNMENT MATURITY MODEL®

Business Results	Isolated Islands	Grudging Cooperation	Benign Agreement	Active Alignment
	LEVEL 1	LEVEL 2	LEVEL 3	LEVEL 4
Individual Mindsets	I succeed by making sure my goals are met.	I'm very busy doing important work in my area.	I agree we should do "that." (I hope someone does it . . .)	I'm part of a leadership team that works together.
Group Dynamics	We meet for status readouts that are boring and repetitive.	We compete with each other for resources and for glory.	We have circular conversations that are polite and respectful, and no one takes action afterward.	We productively disagree, discuss, debate, decide, and take aligned action.

Image 1.3: Karrikins Alignment Maturity Model

Most teams we meet are at level 2, maybe level 3. Unfortunately, level 3 is often the riskiest place to be. It's the level where things feel OK, but misalignment is simmering. The leadership team agrees about what needs to be done, but they aren't doing anything about it. Level 3 is only fine if you are satisfied with the status quo, and your customers, employees, and shareholders don't care about growth. Very few companies can succeed long term in this manner—including yours.

Getting out of the Failure Gap and moving from agreement to alignment takes time, effort, and commitment from leaders who have the courage to give voice to the mindsets and group dynamics that are supporting old patterns, holding back progress, creating havoc, or spinning unnecessary emergencies while reinforcing boundaries that prevent leaders from seeing opportunities and risks in their markets.

If you are willing to have these conversations with your colleagues, *you can be the catalyst for change.* I'm excited to share more about how to do that in the following chapters.

KEY TAKEAWAYS

» When transformations don't deliver the expected ROI, it is often because leaders got stuck in the Failure Gap—the space between agreement and alignment, where good ideas and great intentions go to die.

» There are clear differences between agreement and alignment. Understanding these differences is vital to your business. When your team or company is struggling to move from agreement to alignment, change is impossible.

» Misalignment impacts how teams deliver on strategic objectives, transformation, and market shifts as well as how teams function together in areas like collaboration, innovation, and growth.

» Alignment requires a change in individual mindsets, group dynamics, and organizational structures, among other things. These changes are possible with effort, but teams have to commit the time to work on it together.

» Staying in the Failure Gap means missing opportunities and threats in your marketplace. Businesses fail while leaders are busy doing other things.

» Even seemingly simple things like collaboration fall into the Failure Gap when leaders don't figure out *HOW* to lead together.

Check out www.makehowmatter.com/worksheets
for more resources.

In an ever more digital world, powerful leadership is becoming ever more human.

2

The Karrikins Diamond Triangle: Knowing WHAT and WHY Is Insufficient

Leaders must encourage their organizations to
dance to forms of music yet to be heard.

—Warren Bennis, author, management consultant

THINK ABOUT WHAT HAS HELD your team back from achieving your most ambitious goals. It's very likely you knew WHAT you wanted to do—your strategy, plans, or goals. You probably knew WHY you wanted to do it—your mission, vision, purpose, or a clear call to action. If you struggled to deliver, I'm willing to bet you didn't have clarity on *HOW* to do it together as a team. That's because knowing WHAT and WHY is important, but it is insufficient to propel you forward and across the Failure Gap.

In a world obsessed with WHAT and WHY, *HOW* you lead together makes all the difference.

If you've recognized the signs of the Failure Gap, you and your company's leaders can work together to get aligned and fix the problem by *making HOW matter*. A great way to start is by creating your Diamond Triangle. The Diamond Triangle is a framework that highlights the need to know WHAT you are doing, WHY you are doing it, and *HOW* to lead together to deliver.

We designed the Diamond Triangle framework at Karrikins Group to illustrate the three elements we believe every business needs to articulate in order to move over the Failure Gap and into alignment on their most ambitious goals and highest-order purpose.

Mission
Vision
Purpose
Values

Leadership Ambition

WHY

HOW

Strategy
Initiatives
Priorities
BHAGs

WHAT

Team Commitments

Image 2.1: The Karrikins Diamond Triangle Framework

» The WHAT is your strategy, priorities, plans, and BHAGs (big, hairy, audacious goals as described by Jim Collins in his book *Good to Great*).

» The WHY is your mission, vision, purpose, or call to action.

» The *HOW* is where alignment happens—it is how your ways of leading together bring your WHAT and WHY to life. It includes specific individual mindsets, group dynamics, and organizational factors as well as trade-offs and blockers that drive decision-making and behaviors.

Most teams I work with have a pretty good idea of WHAT they do and WHY, but they don't have clarity on *HOW* to lead together, and it holds them back from success in major initiatives, transformations, integrations, and other market-impacting objectives. The Diamond Triangle helps leadership teams identify where they need more clarity to drive new outcomes for their teams, customers, and businesses.

Remember, knowing WHAT and WHY is important, but they are insufficient for businesses to thrive. You must also know *HOW* to lead together to be exceptional at transformation, drive growth, and deliver results.

Let's take a closer look at each area of the Diamond Triangle, starting with WHAT.

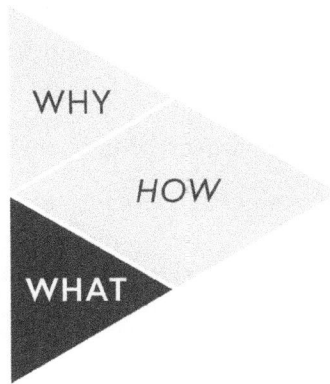

Image 2.2: WHAT Diamond Triangle

WHAT is it that we do?

Here's a quick question for you: Did you wake up today with nothing to do? For most people, the answer is no. In fact, there's more on the list than they can even begin to tackle. That list is the WHAT of the Diamond Triangle. It is the combination of the strategies, goals, projects, tasks, programs, initiatives, and other actions your company or team does to move forward. Your company or team probably has more than enough strategies or priorities to get into the next century. It is very possible you don't need another strategy; you just need to get going on the ones you have, learn along the way, and adjust as you go. Think about your current list of priorities or projects. I'm willing to bet there are plenty on the list. They all represent what you and your team should be doing.

Common items I see on the WHAT list of things to do include:

- » Transform our go-to-market approach
- » Implement a new enterprise resource planning system (ERP) or other significant technology
- » Invest in product innovation
- » Commit to delivering a world-class customer experience
- » Complete a merger or acquisition and successfully integrate the companies
- » Focus on people and culture to address employee concerns
- » Deliver organic growth of 30 percent or more

I'm guessing some of those sound familiar. For some teams, the WHAT might be more specific:

- » Complete a major program or initiative
- » Deploy a new technology or process

» Improve operational metrics or delivery timelines

» Improve customer satisfaction scores

The list is endless for WHAT companies and teams do. The important thing for you to consider is whether or not you and your colleagues are clear on those initiatives and priorities and if you are taking things off the list as well as adding to it. If you do need a better-defined WHAT, that's OK. Thinking about the framework of the Diamond Triangle is meant to help you understand where you have gaps.

If you can't articulate the WHAT of your Diamond Triangle, or you think you don't have the right things on your WHAT list, it is important to address these gaps. Your team needs strategic clarity and connection to move into action. It is also important that everyone across the company has a clear understanding of corporate-level strategies. Teams must share what they are prioritizing in their areas so the organization can move forward together. While developing your *HOW* is the focus of this book, if you find you need more work on your WHAT, consider starting with an inventory of everything that's on the to-do list. Then take a step back and work with your team to see if there are ways to refine, refocus, or prune the list to make sure you are putting effort toward the right things.

We have a Focus on WHAT Matters worksheet on our resources page, and I've often seen teams go through this simple exercise and discover that they could eliminate 10 to 20 percent of their effort pretty quickly by taking the time to do this analysis. It won't solve the lack of a robust strategy, but it may help illuminate some areas for focus and resourcing for what you have today and help you create a placeholder for the WHAT of your Diamond Triangle.

Now let's take a look at the WHY of the Diamond Triangle.

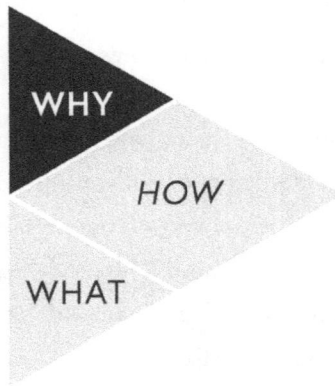

Image 2.3: WHY Diamond Triangle

WHY do we do it?

At the highest level, the WHY of the Diamond Triangle is a prompt for articulating the mission, vision, purpose, and values of your team or organization. The WHY serves as both an anchor and an inspiration for people to keep in mind regarding what it means to be a member of your team and organization. For more operational teams, the WHY could also be a call to action, for example, a board or CEO imperative, market opportunity, or competitive threat. It is helpful to be able to point to these grounding statements when you are bringing team members together and asking them to commit their talent to delivering on priorities and goals.

At a corporate level, the WHY might be expressed as some type of impact statement. For example, Tesla's mission is to accelerate the world's transition to more sustainable energy. Google started with a purpose to organize the world's information and make it universally accessible and useful. General Electric Aerospace's purpose is to invent the future of flight, lift people up, and bring them home safely.

At an operational team level, a WHY might be included in a team charter outlining the purpose and function of the team. At this level, the

WHY is typically narrow and specific to the function of the team. Here are a few examples I've come across:

» **Sales teams:** Our purpose is to connect customers with the right combination of product and services to help them succeed at what they do.

» **Customer support teams:** We aim to provide excellent service to every customer, every time, and to resolve issues as quickly and efficiently as possible so customers can get back to enjoying the benefits our products provide.

» **Operations teams:** Our purpose is to ensure the integrity of our technology platforms while guiding innovation and supporting our colleagues in their use of systems and processes.

» **Transformation teams:** Our mission is to successfully guide the transformation of our organization through diligent planning and execution, consistent support of our colleagues, and continuous monitoring and reporting on our progress while celebrating our successes.

While establishing and understanding your WHY is important, it has unfortunately become more of a marketing exercise than a compelling way to guide behaviors and decision-making. Think about how many disgraced companies have or had "integrity" as a part of their mission, vision, or values. Here's a famous one: Enron. Enron was a large energy company based in Houston, Texas. In December 2001, it declared bankruptcy as a result of an accounting scandal that saw its CEO and CFO convicted on fraud charges that drove the creation of entirely new legislation (Sarbanes–Oxley Act) meant to demand higher accountability from executives. That gives you a good indication of how much influence marketing-designed statements have on leader behaviors.

Similarly, Tyco, a security systems and fire protection company that diversified significantly in the late 1990s, had "integrity" as a published value when it, too, was embroiled in an accounting scandal that almost destroyed the company. In the Tyco case, the CEO and CFO were both convicted of stealing from the company—behavior that was highly misaligned with the company's mission and values. For both Enron and Tyco, there wasn't an understanding of *HOW* to act with integrity. These are extreme examples of higher-order callings run amok, but it isn't unusual for companies to have lofty ideals without the clarity and connection to bring them to life.

In most cases, a WHY relates to motivations, goals, ideals, and branding. It is helpful to have these statements to frame the brand and the organization, whether it is at the corporate level or at a team level. They provide a public touchstone for expectations and aspirations colleagues share, which can help set the tone for the culture, put a human dimension to the brand for customers, and clarify basic expectations of colleagues. However, the WHY can also be calls to action to address a specific moment in time. These might sound like:

- » **Competitive threats:** Why are we transforming? Because we are losing market share to a new competitor, product, or trend, and we need to respond.

- » **Technology expectations:** Our customers and employees expect us to be able to provide technology that is on par with or ahead of others in our space.

- » **Slow or outdated business models:** We aren't keeping up with the market, and our customers are transforming faster than we are, so we are at risk of becoming obsolete.

A risk to these kinds of compelling calls to action is that organizations become immune to them over time if leaders don't align and deliver on them. Think about how often companies talk about transformation or about strategic priorities and then fail to resource them appropriately. When colleagues hear those kinds of declarations often enough, they start to tune them out and stay busy with business as usual. In my opinion, this isn't because they are change-resistant. It's because they've gone on the ride before, only to have it come to a screeching halt when leaders get distracted. So they've learned not to get too engaged—they've been trained to orient toward urgent WHYs with a "this too shall pass" mentality.

When you think about your team or organization, what comes to mind as your WHY? You may have a few things you would include here—a higher-order corporate purpose, a team charter, a business imperative, or possibly just a simple understanding of the impact your team has. The focus of this book is the *HOW*, but you should have a good sense of your WHY as well. For more on building out your WHY, Simon Sinak and others have wonderful resources to explore, several of which are included on our resources page.

WHY statements are important to have and should be gut checked periodically, but they require aligned action from leaders, and that work happens when you lean into creating the *HOW* of the Diamond Triangle. Your WHAT defines the things you are doing, your WHY tells employees and customers the higher-order calling for the work you do, and your *HOW* brings it all into reality by connecting leaders to the hard work of aligning on working together as a leadership team.

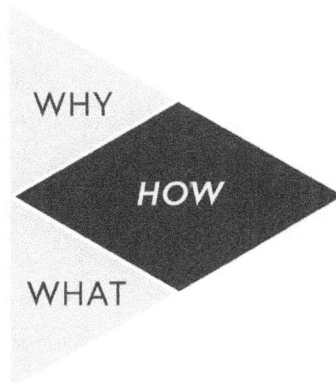

Image 2.4: *HOW* Diamond Triangle

HOW do we do it together?

The reason I wrote this book is because most organizations spend a lot of time and resources on the WHAT and WHY and very little on getting leaders to be clear on *HOW* they will lead together: *HOW* will leaders behave differently and make different decisions that will change the outcomes they deliver? *HOW* will they hold one another accountable to those behaviors and decisions over time? *HOW* do they need to work and lead together to deliver on their WHAT and live up to their WHY? *HOW* do they need to shift their behaviors to bring their biggest ambitions to life?

These are the questions that keep me up at night!

My observation has been that companies spend an extraordinary amount of time, money, and resources developing things like strategies, transformation plans, priorities, missions, visions, purpose statements, and values without any investment in *HOW* the leaders need to lead differently together to deliver the desired outcomes. That's tragic, because the WHAT and the WHY are all about impact, and if you don't deliver on them, you miss the opportunity to do great things in the world. And without a well-defined *HOW*, you are unlikely to deliver as quickly, effectively, and impactfully as you could.

> *HOW*, in the Diamond Triangle, answers the following question: *HOW* will we lead and work together to deliver? It is not the tasks, steps, or actions that make up the detailed execution plan for the WHAT.

Answering the question of *HOW* to lead together is about mindsets, group dynamics, and some of the organizational factors that help leaders take an enterprise view and align with new ways of working together. It forces visibility on often ignored or unspoken trade-offs and blockers that drive leadership behaviors that get in the way of growth and transformation. It's hard work, but when leaders get clear on *HOW* to lead together, they go on to do amazing things.

Here's a visual to help you piece this concept together:

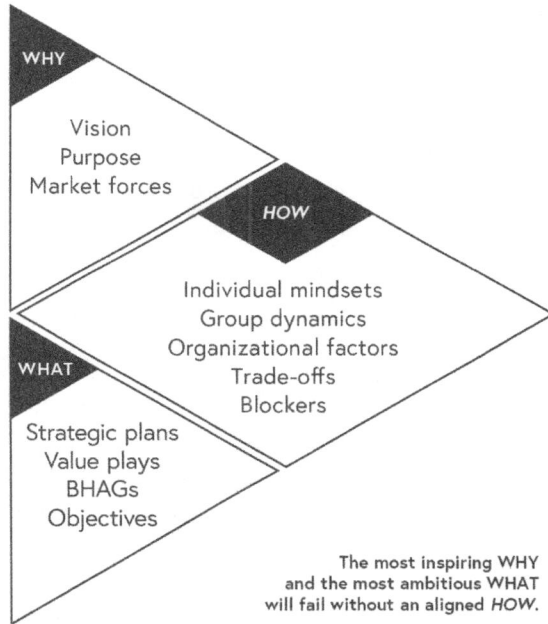

WHY

Vision
Purpose
Market forces

HOW

Individual mindsets
Group dynamics
Organizational factors
Trade-offs
Blockers

WHAT

Strategic plans
Value plays
BHAGs
Objectives

The most inspiring WHY
and the most ambitious WHAT
will fail without an aligned *HOW*.

Image 2.5: Karrikins Diamond Triangle Framework

Don't forget one of the hard truths I mentioned earlier: You and your team need to figure out *HOW* to lead together for yourselves. You can't outsource it to your human resources team, marketing department, or consultants. You have to spend the time in conversation with one another about how you intend to work as a team. Having a structured process to follow and an experienced facilitator for the conversations will accelerate the process and improve your results, but only if you and your team are fully present and doing the work for yourselves. Remember, think of it like going to the gym: Having a trainer is great, but they can't do your reps for you, or they will build muscles, and you won't change at all.

Where to Watch Out for Misalignment

When you don't have a well-articulated *HOW*, it is easy to hit walls or obstacles that push your team or organization into the Failure Gap. These obstacles to alignment show up in a lot of different ways within organizations, but here are some common ones to watch for:

» **"Woulda, coulda, and shoulda"** gets said a lot, but the work doesn't move forward. Have you ever heard "We really should collaborate more" or "If only we would have prioritized better"? How about "We could be more innovative . . ."? When leaders know what needs to be done but struggle to put the plan into action, *woulda*, *coulda*, and *shoulda* do nothing to help.

» **The strategy merry-go-round** is an annual event. Pricey consultants are hired to work with a select group of people to devise the next great strategy. A few months later, the new strategy is rolled out, but it sounds an awful lot like the previous strategy, which never got implemented. Within a quarter, no one talks about the new strategy anymore—and it's back to business as usual.

» **"Nothing to see here" status meetings** are a waste of time. These are usually regular or standing meetings to go through status reports. The only time a department reports anything other than "green" is if the problem is so visible there's no hiding it. You present your status to the team and tune out the rest, thinking, *Nothing exciting happens in these meetings anyway.*

» **Abstract values** are big words with little impact on behavior in the organization. There's a lot of marketing, and absolutely nothing changes in how people work together.

» **The transformation flop** becomes an almost annual joke. For the first month of the year, leaders buzz about the need to transform. By February, everyone is back to business as usual, and the strategies, goals, and ambitions just get rolled into next year.

» **Leaders opt out of changing themselves** and instead focus on changing everyone else. But change doesn't happen while leaders are busy doing other things. People are reluctant to talk about the degree to which leaders in the organization contribute to resistance to change through how they lead, but resistance starts at the top.

» **Organizational factors** get messed with, but they are not the answer. Your company or team is going through its third restructuring of the year, or the processes are getting redesigned for the umpteenth time, and you know nothing will actually change. Because organizational factors are rarely the reason growth isn't happening, transformations fail, or problems persist.

» **Success barriers** are invisible. The only way to define *HOW* to lead together is to have the right conversations about the often-invisible influencers of leader behaviors and decision-making. Nobody is talking about the elephants in the room that are holding back progress because they are human issues, not technology, process, or structure problems.

I'm sure at least a few of these obstacles sound familiar to you. Consider reading them twice and noting the ones that really stand out for you. Each of these reasons has an embedded *HOW* leadership problem associated with it. These problems are only solved when you figure out *HOW* to lead more effectively so the entire team delivers positive business results. As we go through the next few chapters and talk about completing your *HOW*, you can come back to this list and think about how you can apply the tools we are diving into as you work to create shifts around the signals that really resonate with you.

If you've never experienced anything like the above obstacles, you are a unicorn, and I want to meet you—hit me up on LinkedIn. Or, perhaps you are living in a cabin in the woods, writing a manifesto, in which case, don't hit me up on LinkedIn. . . . All joking aside, if you have experienced any of the above scenarios, you are very, very normal. Most people have either observed or participated in one or more of these types of situations throughout their careers. They are pervasive and persistent. They all point to situations where an organization or team has a pretty good idea of their WHAT and their WHY, but they haven't done the work to figure out *HOW* to lead together to deliver on new outcomes. The result, typically, is that they fall short on expected results or fail to deliver altogether.

HOW to lead together is a human-centric question, not a process, structure, or technology one. That's because how we work together is deeply human. But that doesn't mean this work is touchy-feely or just a nice-to-have. Delivering on tough strategies, transformations, and growth requires alignment—business success depends on it. Aligned leaders work to bring clarity and connection to big ambitions and then act with commitment and courage to deliver together, exceed expectations, and create incredible business results.

The Four Cs

As I've worked with leaders around the world, my observation has been that most teams don't have the level of *clarity, connection, commitment,* and *courage* they need to take ground on their WHAT and WHY through a well-established *HOW*. I call these the Four Cs:

> » **Clarity** is all about leaders working together to create a shared understanding of what the expectations and requirements are when it comes to living up to the WHY and delivering the WHAT.

> » **Connection** is about the degree to which leaders understand the whole business and not just their part of it and *HOW* they connect their decisions and behaviors to the broader impacts they have as enterprise leaders.

> » **Commitment** is the shift to new behaviors and decisions that drive different actions at a leadership level.

> » **Courage** is staying true to *HOW* leaders want to lead together to deliver on their most ambitious goals, even when it gets hard.

Here's how we think about the Four *C*s within our Karrikins Alignment Competency Model:

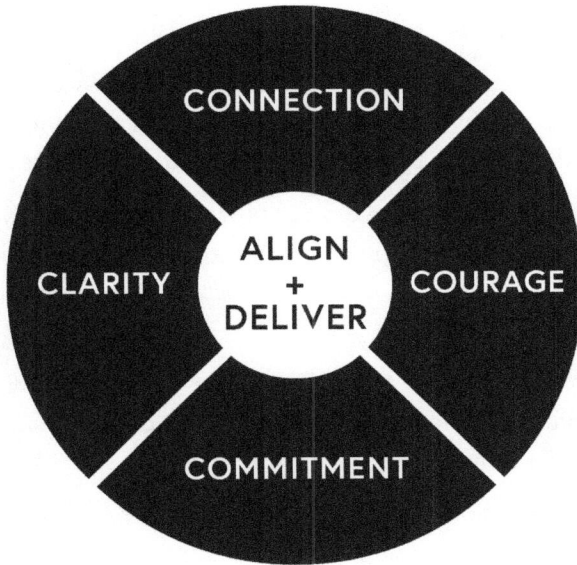

Image 2.6: Karrikins Alignment Competency Model

Working on your *HOW* is difficult. Sometimes it feels risky or time-consuming. It requires getting into tough conversations about your individual mindsets and the group dynamics of your team. People would generally rather leave those things unaddressed. But when they are invisible, they get in the way. They slow down progress, gum up innovation, and prevent priorities from being resourced and delivered.

There are a few reasons I see leaders shy away from doing the work to create *clarity* and *connection*, and then have the *commitment* and *courage* to work as a team. Here are the top seven—some of them might be familiar to you:

1. **Agreement is easy.** Stopping at agreement is easy and feels good. When things are vague enough to be accurate, there's no need for difficult conversations.

2. **Talking feels like it takes too long.** Leaders believe they have far more important things to do than to talk about things they'd rather not discuss.

3. **The status quo seems safer.** Leaders don't see the need to change how they lead, so they don't shift their individual mindsets. It's easier to focus on changing others instead.

4. **Organizational factors feel more real.** Leaders work on organizational factors like organizational charts and compensation plans, expecting processes and systems to fix human problems.

5. **Silos feel comfortable.** The success of their vertical area feels within individual control and is a higher priority than working together to make sure the organization succeeds.

6. **Mindsets and group dynamics are hard to identify.** It is uncomfortable and feels risky to talk about the real barriers to progress when they are so deeply human.

7. **There's a belief in objective decision-making.** Leaders believe they are making objective decisions when they encounter trade-offs, but they are often making deeply habituated ones that are influenced by subjective factors.

There's no doubt that figuring out *HOW* to lead and work together is hard work. But answer these questions: Is it harder than creating an amazing strategy that never gets implemented? Or knowing you need to transform but getting stuck and watching your competition fly by you? Or seeing employees leave because they have lost confidence in leadership? Because those aren't just hard; they are heartbreaking.

Clarity, connection, commitment, and *courage* can do wonders for establishing the alignment required between you and your fellow leaders as you move through the Failure Gap and deliver on big, ambitious strategies. I know you can get there, and the tools and resources in this book will help you on your way.

As we move forward together through the following sections, we will break down the different elements of your *HOW* and share examples, scenarios, and ways of engaging your colleagues in conversations that will help you to build out the Diamond of your Diamond Triangle.

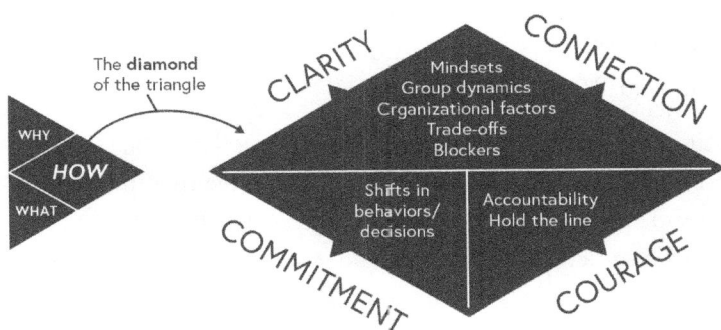

Image 2.8: The Diamond of the Triangle

Throughout this book, you'll notice the exercises and associated resources are geared toward helping you have the conversations you need to establish *HOW* to lead together with your colleagues. The more you do together, the stronger your *HOW* will become. The stronger your *HOW*, the more success that you, your team, and your business will enjoy.

So far we've talked about taking an inventory of where you are stuck in agreement, noticing and naming those situations, and self-assessing. These are all great starting points for discussion with your colleagues and teams. In the next section, we'll get deeper into the conversations you need to have to build out your Diamond and unlock your team's full potential, especially when tackling a big transformation effort!

KEY TAKEAWAYS

» In a world obsessed with WHAT and WHY, *HOW* you lead together makes all the difference. The Karrikins Diamond Triangle is a framework that highlights the need to know WHAT you are doing, WHY you are doing it, and *HOW* to lead together to deliver.

» In the Diamond Triangle, WHAT defines your strategies, priorities, transformation plans, projects, programs, and other work you do. WHY defines your mission, purpose, vision, values, and compelling calls to action. *HOW*, which is often the missing piece, defines how you intend to lead or work together to deliver on your WHAT and your WHY.

» It is important to know your WHAT and WHY, but they are insufficient to create the leader behaviors required to drive your team and business forward. This is usually where leaders experience misalignment. *HOW* to lead and work together is the secret to building the alignment required for new outcomes.

» Outside support can create the time and structure needed for quality conversations to define your *HOW*, but ultimately, you and your colleagues must put in the effort to create positive change.

» *Clarity, connection, commitment,* and *courage* are required to avoid the Failure Gap and succeed through a well-established *HOW*.

Check out www.makehowmatter.com/worksheets
for more resources.

Transformations fail while leaders are busy doing more important things.

3

Tackling Transformations: The Struggle Is Real

The only way you survive is you continuously transform into something else. It's this idea of continuous transformation that makes you an innovation company.

—Ginni Rometty, former CEO of IBM

FRUSTRATIONS AROUND ALIGNMENT ARE WIDESPREAD—the desire to be more transformative, innovative, or customer focused is common, especially on enterprise-level teams. Taking the time to bring clarity and connection to *HOW* to lead together in new ways closes the behavioral gap that keeps teams stuck in agreement. We're going to get into an approach for doing that in the next section.

Before we go there, let's consider the risks introduced by leaving your *HOW* blank when the gap between agreement and alignment involves even higher stakes than a localized challenge, like collaborating across a team. Think about when a company has big strategic goals to reach or a massive *transformation* to deliver. Despite the common excuse of the doers in an organization resisting or fearing change, what I've seen is that misaligned leadership is a root cause of many failed investments in transformations including the integration of a merger/acquisition, a new product or market expansion, a significant restructuring, a new go-to-market strategy that impacts customers as well as colleagues, or a massive technology lift.

One of the most common transformations companies attempt these days relates to technology platforms. I work with many companies who need to consolidate their systems. One client of ours reported having sixteen-plus instances of a cloud-based customer relationship management (CRM) technology platform. CRMs are designed to help streamline and improve the customer experience and make it easier to manage customer relationships across a complex organization. Having many different versions of the same application risks creating the opposite situation—it introduces complexity, redundant work for salespeople, and confusion for customers.

Another client had forty-two different enterprise resource planning (ERP) system implementations scattered across three continents. ERPs are designed to manage the operations of a business—all the day-to-day functions like accounting, finance, procurement, human resources, compliance, and other business-critical activities. Each of the forty-two purchasing decisions those ERPs represented might have made sense in isolation, but when you step back and look at the enterprise as a whole, it makes it very difficult to streamline, scale, and leverage all of the investments being made across niche areas of the company. The really crazy thing is, those two examples are on the low side!

So many of the efforts and investments in technology solutions are well documented in terms of WHAT needs to be done and WHY. A lot of time, money, and effort goes into building beautiful PowerPoint slides and posters to explain the transformation. In the best-case scenario, town halls are held, emails go out, training is conducted, and each individual senior leader does their part in their area to sponsor the transformation. But, because senior leaders don't invest in getting granular about *HOW* to lead the transformation together and *HOW* they need to change themselves, the work falters, and all the money and effort put into the WHAT and WHY fails to convert into the desired ROI. Leaders tend to blame the people who *do* the work, not the people who *lead* the work—they talk about a "change-resistant culture" without an acknowledgment of how influential leaders are when it comes to setting the standard for a changeable culture.

As transformation efforts get organized, rolled out, and then steam-rolled by business as usual, the organization learns to be wary of them. We call this "the flop," or sometimes "the whiplash" effect, which is when the same transformation is attempted year after year with the same dismal results. There's a visual on the following page so you see how these play out.

In these transformation energy maps, you can see that when a transformation effort is announced and a kickoff happens, leader energy is very high. Leader energy represents the time, attention, and personal commitment leaders are demonstrating to achieve the goals of the transformation.

If you aren't transforming your leadership, you aren't transforming your company.

Then, leader energy takes a dive because the gravitational pull of business as usual takes over. Leaders go back to their "day jobs," and the transformation becomes something someone else is doing—responsibility has been outsourced to a transformation lead, a change-management team, or a consultant.

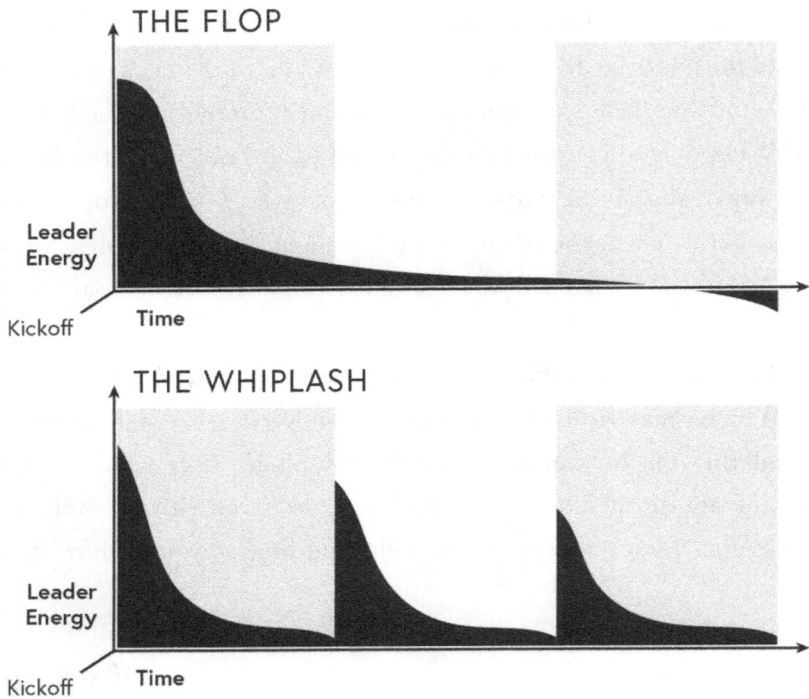

THE FLOP

Leader Energy

Kickoff   Time

THE WHIPLASH

Leader Energy

Kickoff   Time

Image 3.1: Typical Transformation Energy Maps

Maybe you've been at a company that has gone through the flop or fallen into the whiplash cycle—it is pretty common. Have you ever wondered how it is possible to spend so much money and still come up short? I've worked on more than one of these efforts, and it typically isn't about the technology or change management for the people in the organization. It's a failure at the senior leadership level, a misalignment on *HOW* they need to lead differently to successfully transform. If you aren't transforming your leadership, you aren't transforming your company.

Leader Activation and Change Management

Leader alignment and activation during transformation are very different from change management that is targeted at the workers in the organization. *Change management* is all about changing how people work. *Leader activation* is about aligning how leaders lead. In the language of alignment, leader activation is in the *HOW*, and change management is in the WHAT—the difference between how leaders lead and what workers do.

Consider this example. Suppose an engineering company that makes custom manufacturing equipment decides to change its go-to-market approach. Instead of just selling products, it wants to bundle in services, too. That means the company's salespeople need to learn how to sell a more complex package that takes longer to close but yields higher revenue and margin. Change management will help the salespeople learn the new processes, pitches, and customer specifications so they know what to do differently in their jobs. Good sponsorship of change management means that leaders send out periodic updates that the change-management team writes for them, they are supportive of their salespeople attending training, and they engage with the rewards and recognition program the change-management team puts together. That's awesome and important, but it isn't enough to drive implementation of the new go-to-market strategy, because being a sponsor of other people's changes isn't enough to transform an organization. Leaders must also change how they lead.

Leader activation ensures senior leaders learn how to guide the sales teams, set different types of sales targets, and create different language for sales. In this example, leaders who have built their careers based on their engineering expertise need to learn to work with peers who specialize in services. If the transformation to a sales and service go-to-market plan is successful, it will include very different solutions than what the leaders are used to discussing, so they will need to be fluent in the new packaging. There might be new reports to understand, a new set of terms to adopt, and new ways of measuring success. Leaders have to take on the work of learning all these new things if they want to align and transform their organizations.

Put simply, leader activation makes sure leaders are showing up for the transformation and not staying stuck in old ways of leading—changing *HOW* they lead. Change management helps the doers in the organization learn new skills, processes, and technology to help them succeed—changing WHAT they do.

Here's a side-by-side comparison of the two so you can see these important distinctions:

LEADER ACTIVATION	CHANGE MANAGEMENT
Sustaining visible leadership energy and focus	Developing the **message platform**
Building fluency in new business language	Building **communication plans**
Changing the questions being used to evaluate	Establishing the **timeline and road map**
Challenging legacy mindsets and beliefs	Coordinating **across teams**
Modeling the way for others	Managing **training** development and delivery
Creating the space for connections to be made	Tracking **progress for the transformation**

Image 3.2: Leader Activation and Change Management

Take a look at the differences between leader activation and change management. If you think about a transformation effort you've experienced, where did most of the resources go? Probably toward the right side, not the left. It is a very common situation, and one that I'm on a personal mission to address through the work of *making HOW matter.*

Imagine for a moment that your leaders were fully *activated* during a transformation instead of just sponsoring change management. Wouldn't that make a difference in the success or failure of the effort? Remember, in the language of the Diamond Triangle, change management focuses on

WHAT people do, and leader activation is all about *HOW* leaders lead together to deliver.

Completing your Diamond Triangle during transformation helps leaders define *HOW* to stay energized and activated together. It allows you and your company leaders to create clarity and connection regarding how to maintain what we call a "successful simmer" throughout the program and long after the organization has successfully moved on to a new modality. When leaders do the work to build shared meaning around *HOW* to lead together and then put intentional effort behind that, they transform their organizations better, faster, and with a more reliable ROI.

The chart below shows another version of the transformation energy map, one where leaders are maintaining a successful simmer.

Leading the ideal transformation by maintaining a "successful simmer" of leader activation means:
- Leaders set the tone and remain visibly engaged
- Leader energy ebbs and flows instead of spiking and cratering
- Leaders become fluent in the language of the future

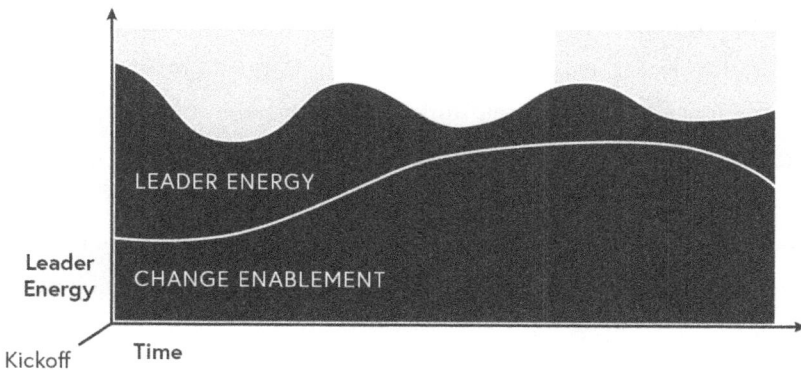

Image 3.3: Transformation Successful Simmer Map

Unlike the flop or the whiplash, this chart shows what happens when leader energy keeps up a successful simmer over the course of the transformation effort. Remember that leader energy represents the time, attention, and personal commitment leaders are demonstrating to the goals of the transformation. When a successful simmer is maintained, leaders never fully go back to their day jobs. While they can't stay energetically at the level they had at kickoff, they never fall back down into business as usual either. Instead, they stay actively engaged throughout the transformation by visibly demonstrating their own change as leaders, focusing on their own behaviors and decision-making processes. By the end, they have established a new baseline for their habituated leadership activities.

Let's go back to the earlier example of a go-to-market transformation where the sales force needs to start selling services in addition to products. Leaders who are energetically activated in the transformation will start using the new language of sales instead of staying stuck in the old vocabulary. So, when the quarterly reports come around, they might ask salespeople to share what percentage of their total quota was met through services and dig into understanding the new sales velocity metrics that reflect the reality of moving a more complex sale through the pipeline. Leaders can start asking curious questions about what's getting in the way of bundling in services and helping salespeople to think through the approach and resources they need. When leaders are energetically engaged, they set the tone and maintain the focus required to transform the organization. When they aren't engaged, they cling to the past in their language and thinking, evaluating success based on dated metrics and failing to demonstrate an advanced understanding of the transformed business model, and everyone takes the cue and settles back into business as usual, slowing transformation efforts or halting them altogether.

When leaders align to maintain a successful simmer throughout a transformation, it fundamentally changes the trajectory of the effort. Imagine if you and your leadership team were able to ebb and flow your energy without flopping completely—you'd get where you are going faster, with less investment, and with engaged and enthusiastic colleagues.

Awesome, right?

Take another look at the transformation energy charts. Compare the transformation energy map showing a successful simmer to the transformation energy map showing the flop or the whiplash. Which one do you relate to the most in terms of your experiences with organizational transformation? Check in with your colleagues and ask them about their experiences with transformations your company has worked through. Find out what they have seen and what you can learn from that about how leaders are leading.

When Misalignment Hits

Let's take a closer look at how misalignment happens during transformations, and why senior leaders must tackle the work of *HOW* to lead together. The experiences of a company we'll call SnackInvasion are representative of many very real experiences I've had with companies going through transformation.

Let's say SnackInvasion was a multinational consumer packaged goods (CPG) firm with a complex supply chain and distribution model, all tuned for pre-Covid-19 realities. When Covid-19 hit in 2020, they had to make massive adjustments just to survive in an unprecedented environment. In 2023, as things started to normalize, they realized they needed to avoid falling back into the same old ways of working that dominated pre-Covid-19. But they also needed to avoid normalizing the craziness of the during-Covid-19 reality. They needed a new normal, and part of that was fully committing to transforming their ERP infrastructure. They'd attempted it several times prior to Covid-19 and then put it on the back burner while they navigated that situation. Unfortunately, the company's infrastructure contained seventeen different ERP systems and many different versions of those seventeen systems, so consolidation and rationalization were the first orders of business.

The CEO (who we'll call Jordon) and the CFO (who we'll call Sandy) both realized the enormity of the challenge. In fact, it had been tried in the past to no avail—millions of dollars and untold hours had been invested in failed efforts to consolidate even just a few of the systems. At least two CEOs had lost their jobs over failed ERP consolidation efforts at Snack-Invasion, and they'd been through five CIOs in as many years. Sandy was a survivor, going through it all in a twenty-plus-year career with the company. She made it clear she wasn't going to lose her job over this one, either. Others on the executive team, including the regional presidents, felt the same way. As a fairly new CEO, Jordon wasn't keen on suffering the same fate as his predecessors and felt the pressure to get moving quickly on what promised to be a long and difficult effort.

For Jordon and his SnackInvasion leadership team, the WHAT and the WHY were always clear. At a high level, they sounded like this:

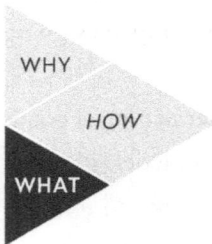

"We need to eliminate overlap, reduce duplication of effort and spending, and simplify our business so we can respond more quickly to changing market conditions globally," said Jordon. "This will help our customers do business with us in different regions without unnecessary complexity. And, it will enable employees who work across regions to be more effective. That means we must reduce the number of ERP systems we support while creating consistent processes and data across our geographies.

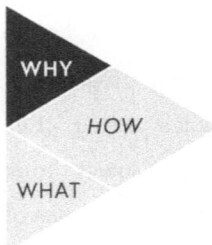

"For us to fulfill our mission and deliver on our purpose, we need to simplify, streamline, and consolidate systems," Jordon added, addressing his leadership team. "Our environment is too complex and hard for employees and customers to navigate. We spend too much money on similar or duplicate systems, and we can't leverage people, practices, or data across geographies in our current situation. This holds us back from doing our best in delivering high-quality, accessible, and fun-to-eat snacks around the world."

The entire executive team agreed. They understood the company's WHAT and WHY and that the current environment was holding them back. They all agreed to be sponsors of the transformation and get their people involved in the effort.

But it all sounded painfully familiar, and year after year, the transformation efforts had floundered or failed. The organization was trained to expect the whiplash effect—leaders would get all excited and then the energy would die off. Legacy priorities would kick in, and the transformation would either quietly die away or go out in an explosion of executive dismissals.

They had missed an important step in the past. They hadn't taken the time to answer the question: How are we going to lead differently to transform our organization?

As a result, when things got hard with the transformation effort, the leaders didn't respond in ways that took the organization forward. Instead, they relied on old habits and ways of working to preserve the status quo and maintain reliability in their own areas. The senior leaders were the ones who got in the way of success! It wasn't the systems integrators—they could get their software working in any environment. It wasn't the "doers" in the organization—they were willing to learn new systems and processes. And it wasn't the change-management effort—the trainings, communications, and messaging had always been solid. The problem rested squarely with the most senior leaders in the company.

Here's what kept happening at SnackInvasion, and if you've ever attempted an ERP consolidation (I've been involved in quite a few), this will likely sound familiar. It started with a big bang—the board approved a massive contract for a world-class systems integrator to come in and help with the transformation. The leadership team heard all about it and agreed the business case was sound—the WHAT and the WHY made sense. Then the systems integrator started the work and had one-on-one conversations with each of the regional presidents. Here's a sampling of what they heard:

» **Region A:** "We have a process that works well in our region, a process that runs on a fairly industry-standard ERP system. This is the targeted platform for consolidation."

» **Region B:** "We have a highly customized version of the same ERP system, and over the years we've created specialized workflows and reports that helped drive our business. We have a thousand reasons why the industry-standard processes won't work for us. Our customized version is better for us, and we can't move over to Region A's version of the system. You (the systems integrator) will have to figure out how to crosswalk the data for us so we can still get what we need for our region."

» **Region C:** "We are the smallest region, so we don't get a lot of support. We've implemented our own ERP system that is entirely different from Region A or B. We implemented it ten years ago when the region's president got tired of waiting for the centralized IT team to help. She contracted with an outside company, and the system is relatively inexpensive. It works well enough, and we're satisfied with how it supports our region."

At this point, the company sent the systems integrator to bring the subject matter experts (SMEs) from all three regions into a process design session to duke it out. The SMEs dutifully showed up and participated, but behind the scenes, here's what was playing out:

» **Region A SMEs:** "I'm not sure why I'm even here. . . . Every time we attempt this, I explain why our platforms and processes are the obvious choice. There's nothing for me to really do differently."

» **Region B SMEs:** "We've notified our region's president about our concerns and issues with having to migrate to Region A's processes. There's no way we can make that work."

» **Region C SMEs:** "We'll attend, but remain largely disengaged in the design sessions. The last time this was attempted, the systems integrator gave up because our ERP couldn't do a data migration into the new system, and the cost of conversion was too high. And anyway, our president has assured us our systems aren't changing anytime soon."

When it became clear the transformation was in jeopardy, the regional presidents got involved. After a lot of wrangling at a leadership level, they had the following opinions:

» **Region A president:** "I can't afford to carry the costs of the smaller regions being on my platform, so I've decided we should maintain our existing as-is system, and they can work with the systems integrator to figure out their own needs."

» **Region B president:** "I'll tell my SMEs that the integrator will be instructed to customize the new system to accommodate the workflows they are used to using. We need to focus on hitting our targets, and we can't spend more time trying to figure this out."

» **Region C president:** "Well, I'm clearly not going to do anything until this mess is straightened out, so I'm going to tell my people to stand down and carry on with what we have. We'll come back to it once the dust settles between Regions A and B."

Of course, the customizations for Region B required a change order for the increase in time and cost and, after a bloated and rocky conversion effort, at best, they ended up with a weirdly customized ERP implementation that couldn't possibly be sustained in the long term. At worst, they had a failed investment, with millions of dollars and thousands of hours lost . . . yet again.

Why does this transformation failure happen over and over again? Without a clear answer to *HOW* executives are going to lead together, the presidents all agree with the WHAT and the WHY and then make *individually sensical* but *collectively nonsensical* decisions that materially impact the transformation effort. When these discussions reach the executive level, the regional leaders feel justified in their actions. They might lead from positions like:

» **Region A president:** "We're feeling a lot of pressure over budgets. We naturally want to ensure we don't end up absorbing the costs associated with the smaller regions coming on the platform. Why should we take on additional costs that only hurt our ability to make our numbers? Region A always hits its targets."

» **Region B president:** "I'm proud to have my people's backs, defending their local needs. I'm not going to let them be negatively impacted by this transformation by having to do extra work. The systems integrator is just going to have to figure it out."

» **Region C president:** "This too shall pass. Changes will only increase costs in our region, and we have more important things to focus on, like hitting revenue targets. Perhaps we will get involved later, once the kinks are ironed out. The change-management team is just going to have to wait until then to engage with us."

Sound familiar? These are default ways of leading specific to the regional needs. They get justified in terms of protecting budgets, time, and people and putting the onus on others—the systems integrators, the change-management team, or the doers in the company—to figure it out.

Please understand, I get it—there are all sorts of reasons why consolidating systems is a tough exercise. Local processes are required by specific regional regulations, the influence of a large regional client, or other quirks that are very real and pressing. But it is also true that a lot of objections and resistance points start with the most senior leader being unwilling to lead differently. When the most senior leaders aren't taking on the responsibility of asking new questions, challenging legacy processes, learning new ways of working, and changing how they do business, the organization will remain in the Failure Gap of transformation—with complete *agreement* that it is a good idea and no *alignment* to lead differently together.

This happens all the time—not just with ERP implementations. It happens with reorganizations, with acquisitions, with sales or go-to-market transformation—you name it; if the transformation requires massive, company-wide change, agreeing to WHAT and WHY is insufficient. Senior leaders must align on *HOW* to lead together differently and how to challenge themselves to respond differently when they need to make trade-offs or work through blockers.

I wish I could say the above SnackInvasion case study is based on a real company. The truth is, it isn't just one company. It is based on hundreds of real companies, and the story as described is consistent with ones I have faced with many clients over the years.

Like SnackInvasion, most companies and teams understand the WHY and the WHAT yet fall far short on *HOW* to lead together. When misalignment hits, remember the Diamond Triangle and that the *HOW* bridges the WHAT and the WHY, filling the empty space—the Failure Gap—so positive transformation can happen.

If you are in a situation like SnackInvasion, and your organization is facing massive challenges or opportunities you need to address to transform, it's time to lean in and do the work to complete your Diamond Triangle.

> Avoid the Failure Gap by completing your Diamond Triangle.

The Power of Intentional Dialogue

As one of my favorite clients keenly observed, "This isn't about creating another list of things to do; it's about how we do everything we do." He made that comment when we were working with his team to define their

HOW, and the team was worried they were just going to end up with yet another list of tasks to do or an idealized list of values. He's exactly right. The reason we were spending time together as a team in conversation about what things meant is because "words create worlds," as Abraham Joshua Heschel has said. Through dialogue, our goal was to create enough shared understanding of how to work together that it would become engrained into how they did everything. That's the power of intentional dialogue, which is at the heart of creating your *HOW*.

> Through dialogue, we create a shared understanding of how to interpret and act on new ways of working.

I get it—you are already in so many meetings. The thought of doing something that requires more talking feels daunting. But intentional dialogue is the only way to build a *HOW* that works to align the team to deliver together. Intentional dialogue is creating the space for the right quality conversations to happen so you and your colleagues arrive at a consistent, shared understanding of *HOW* to work and lead together.

Intentional dialogue includes specific conversations about the mindsets, group dynamics, trade-offs, blockers, and shifts that leaders need to commit to in order to successfully lead transformation. I'm going to share more about those elements later, but for now, I want you to anchor in your mind that alignment requires conversations between human beings—not slides, not emails, not spreadsheets. Those may help support dialogue, but they don't replace the need to spend time in conversation.

I realize you might not like hearing that. Perhaps you don't even believe me, and that's OK. I don't take it personally; I realize people are very busy doing very important things. But answer these questions: How often have you belatedly realized that your colleagues aren't on the same page as you, and if only you'd known sooner, you could have gotten where you are going faster and for less investment? Why do you suppose you weren't on the same page? I doubt you needed any more analysis or documentation. You likely needed more conversation to build clarity and connection.

When you are in a conversation with intentional dialogue designed to create clarity and connection to shared goals, emphasize the importance of *talking, not telling* when it comes to defining *HOW* to work together.

» *Talking* is when two or more people share their ideas, concerns, and objections while staying curious about what other people think. Talking provides the space for context to be set and for alignment to be explored.

» *Telling* is one-way communication (instructions, reports, or directions, for example) that often lacks the context and meaning that come from conversation that helps people understand and align to deliver.

Let's think about intentional dialogue and the difference between talking and telling through an example. Teams and organizations often do an exercise where they create values—the WHY of the Diamond Triangle. Every year, reports come out across the web about the most common values, and they inevitably include words like *trust, integrity*, and, you guessed it, *collaboration. Innovation* is usually up there, too. Although trust, integrity, collaboration, and innovation are really good aspirations, they are too abstract to impact behaviors and decision-making. People can only make sense of them in a consistent way if they take the time to engage in intentional dialogue, talking about how to act in ways that align their behaviors to those values.

If you suspect talking sounds like it takes time and effort, you are right. I'm an introvert, so for me, it is especially challenging, but I know, as the CEO of Karrikins Group, it is vitally important—I have to stay in conversation with my colleagues to keep us all aligned to our shared ways of working and goals. It might come as a relief to hear that not everything has to be talked through—this work is for the big ideas, strategies, concepts, and goals about which everyone needs to have a shared understanding. When it comes to your WHAT and your WHY and all the great value you want to create in the world, I'm going to speculate that there's space in your organization for leaders to do more talking and less telling.

I use the following Intentional Dialogue worksheet to help me think about topics I need to talk about with my team. Take a look and see what comes to mind for you. Refer to the worksheet, and write your thoughts here or elsewhere. Then, have a conversation with your team about it.

INTENTIONAL DIALOGUE

Use the Intentional Dialogue worksheet to prepare for conversations where you need to help your colleagues to make sense of an abstract, difficult, or strategic topic.

What is the topic I need to discuss?
• Describe the topic and note any supporting materials

Key points to explore together
•
•
•
•

How can I help my colleagues to make sense of this topic?	How can I help my colleagues to articulate the impact on them/their teams?
• Prompt 1	• Prompt 1
• Prompt 2	• Prompt 2
• Prompt 3	• Prompt 3

Conversation takeaways:
What are our ideas about how we can do this together?
•
•
•

Image 3.4: Intentional Dialogue Worksheet

Here's a simple example of how I might do this with my team if I needed to talk with them about retiring some old templates and using new ones. This might seem like something I should just tell them to do, but in our work, it has big implications for how they deliver to clients and for how we maintain our brand standards. I might fill out the Intentional Dialogue worksheet something like this:

» **What is the topic I need to discuss?**

Switching to new templates for our delivery work.

» **What are the most important points for people to understand?**

This is urgent, so we can maintain our brand standards and consistency in how we deliver to clients, and it will make their jobs easier by making sure they have easy-to-use documents to support their work.

» **How could I frame three questions that would help them to make sense of this topic for themselves?**

1. What's frustrating for you about the templates we are using today?

2. How are you working around those frustrations? (I want to understand their habits and what they are comfortable doing—the devil they know. It may be frustrating, but they know how to navigate it.)

3. What would you have to do differently to migrate to new templates?

» **How can I prompt them to use their own words to articulate the key points and identify the impact on them?**

Let's take a look at the new templates—do they address some of those frustrations?

What's exciting to you about the new template? What makes you nervous?

» **What are my ideas to share about "how we can do this together"?**

I will commit to being available to help them work through the new templates the first few times they use them.

I'll share my own challenges with not going back to old files as a starting point and instead using the new templates and building them out fresh.

We can work together when we are planning a new project kickoff to make sure we are all accessing the new templates and sharing information consistently.

We can help one another shift our mindsets from *This is an extra step* to *This is a necessary and helpful step.*

All of this will take more time than me simply telling them that this is what they need to do and where the templates are, but it will be far more impactful in shifting their patterns and habits into new ways of working with our content; at the end of the day, that will be both faster and more effective. In the opening of this book, I shared that to go far fast, you should get aligned. This is where you see that difference starting to take shape.

The good news is, once you've developed the skill of engaging in intentional dialogue to bring clarity and connection to your WHAT, WHY, and *HOW*, your team will start working differently together on all sorts of things. Meetings will be more productive and enjoyable because you will be using a shared language to make decisions quickly and effectively. Change management will be easier because people will work from a place of understanding instead of compulsion as they model the way being set by leaders who are fully activated. And transformation will start to take hold because people are orienting differently toward how they work together.

In the next section, I'm going to share the Karrikins Behavior Model. This model serves as a more comprehensive guide for intentional dialogue. It will help you and your team build shared meaning around *HOW* you want to lead together. Before we go there, though, let's revisit SnackInvasion and what they need to fill in the missing piece of their Diamond Triangle.

CASE STUDY

Transformation's Missing Piece at SnackInvasion

Jordon and Sandy at SnackInvasion needed to cross the Failure Gap by defining and implementing the *HOW* of their Diamond Triangle as it related to making tough decisions together about consolidation efforts. Similar to Sara's TT1, there was a lot of agreement around the need for SnackInvasion to transform, but they hadn't invested the time to align the senior leaders to lead together. Jordon and Sandy, together with the rest of the executive leaders, needed to build alignment by working together to create:

» An understanding of the mindsets, group dynamics, and organizational factors that influenced their decisions and behaviors

» A grasp of the deeply embedded organizational beliefs that were holding back progress

» A shared language to discuss the trade-offs and obstacles that inevitably arose

» A way to make the invisible visible and to have authentic conversations about how to deliver together

» Defined ways of working together to navigate the leadership of the transformation, including how to negotiate tough choices that would impact all of them in different ways

» A shared desire for new or different outcomes so history was not repeated

» Expectations of one another as leaders who were willing to visibly model the way for the organization

All of this requires *intentional dialogue*—spending time talking together about the often-invisible influences that cement the status quo and hold back aligned action.

Remember that *HOW* is the glue between WHAT and WHY, driving aligned action. By spending time getting clear and specific on *HOW* to lead together on both the WHAT and the WHY, your leadership team will increase the speed with which it can respond to opportunities and threats and exponentially increase the effectiveness of deploying resources and having an impact. It keeps leaders on point for making decisions that align with the goals of the company while helping them support one another when things get hard. The approach you take to defining *HOW* to lead together helps provoke the required action to bring transformational change to life. Let's get into that in the next section!

KEY TAKEAWAYS

» If you are undertaking a big transformation effort, knowing WHAT you are doing and WHY you are doing it is insufficient. You must also know *HOW* to do it together as a team.

» Leader energy during times of transformation often flops as leaders go back to business as usual after a big kickoff event. This trains your organization to expect leaders to check out, leading to a whiplash effect.

» You have likely seen leaders who mistakenly believe that being good sponsors of change management is enough for them to support transformation. Sponsorship is not enough. Leaders must activate their own transformation in how they lead to maintain a successful simmer throughout a transformation effort.

» You need to spend time having intentional dialogue with your colleagues to build a shared understanding of your WHAT and your WHY if you want to align to deliver new outcomes.

» Intentional dialogue takes time, and you can't shortcut it by telling people things. You need to talk with them consistently over time and continue to reinforce what you and your colleagues need to do differently.

» You will find that this work becomes easier as you and your colleagues get good at having *HOW* to lead together conversations.

Check out www.makehowmatter.com/worksheets
for more resources.

PART 2

Leading Better Together

Nothing changes until someone
changes, and that someone
is probably you.

4

The Karrikins Behavior Model: Making the Invisible Visible

If you do not change direction, you may end up where you are going.

—Lao Tzu, Chinese philosopher

BOTH TT1 AND SNACKINVASION ARE examples of teams struggling with alignment. They knew WHAT they should do and WHY they should do it. But they weren't clear on *HOW* to do it together. The struggle to answer the question of *HOW* to lead together is relevant to so many situations in the workplace, ranging from seemingly simple (but actually quite hard) things like collaborating better all the way to getting to the promised ROI on massive transformations like ERP implementations.

You might even see your own team in TT1 or SnackInvasion. Many teams struggle with breaking out of unhelpful routines or ways of working that hold them back from success. Here's the important thing to remember: Just like an individual who is trying to break a habit, your team isn't permanently stuck. You are just repeating patterns of behaviors and decision-making that have worked well for you in the past, hoping for the same results in an environment that has changed. You get unstuck by understanding those patterns and working to adapt them to new conditions.

The Challenge of Habits

Habituated behaviors influence individuals and teams in fascinating ways. I'm not going to get too deep into the research here—there is plenty of literature available on individual habits. If you've never read Charles Duhigg's foundational book *The Power of Habit*, I strongly suggest you give it a read. *Tiny Habits* by BJ Fogg is a great resource for the power of small things done consistently over time, which is a mantra of ours as well. James Clear's exploration in *Atomic Habits* is a recent hit. These are wonderful resources if you are interested in digging into your deeply habituated behaviors and decisions and how you might change them. Spoiler alert: It's hard work! But there are great tools and approaches for helping you to be successful at it. With our work at Karrikins Group, we leverage these seminal works and others to help us build tools and resources to partner effectively with teams of people who are entrenched in habituated ways of working together.

Here's what's good to know: Habits are absolutely phenomenal tools that humans use to make life easier in general. Did you know that research has consistently shown that the average adult makes about 35,000 decisions a day? That's everything from what to have for breakfast to whether to spend $10 million on a new technology platform. Habits help us by streamlining our thinking and making some decisions easier than others.

By defaulting to habituated responses, we can reduce decision fatigue and speed up our response time. That's awesome for a lot of situations, but keep in mind what Kaiser and Kaplan warn against in their book *Fear Your Strengths*—there is such a thing as overusing an individual strength. In a similar vein, the strengths of habituated responses can become barriers to progress when they hold people back from seeing opportunities or mitigating risks. This is especially true when habits are amplified across groups.

The Influence of Organizational Habits

A few years ago, I was working with a team of product managers who were trying to move into a more standard approach to product development and delivery. They were in a life-sciences firm that had grown quickly thanks to patents on some highly specialized equipment. They had a few big clients who had very specific implementations of their solutions. The company wanted to scale more into the mid-market. But scaling would require more standardization, making it harder for the salespeople who were in the habit of customizing every pitch to close a deal.

I have a vivid memory of being in a meeting with the product team, talking about a tighter process for approving specialized orders. The idea was to add hurdles to make it harder for the sales team to write a contract for a custom solution and to encourage them to use more standard solutions. A team member, Robert, leaned back from the table and said, "I don't know why we are even talking about this. We all know what's going to happen. We are going to design this standardization process, and then as soon as a salesperson has a big fish on the line, we're going to get told we have to build something custom. We are just wasting our time."

He wasn't wrong. That's exactly what had happened in the past, and it was likely to happen again. The salespeople were deeply habituated to creating custom solutions for customers. The senior leaders were deeply habituated to approving those customizations to facilitate client acquisition and meet quarterly sales targets. And the product team felt powerless to push back because the company revolved around revenue, even if it came at a terrible margin, which was also a deeply engrained dynamic.

The issue, for Robert, wasn't the lack of a process for approving custom solutions. He was right—no amount of process would change how the salespeople were selling or what the leadership team was approving unless their ways of working changed first. Everyone agreed that growth was good, margins were important, and that standardization was the right goal. But when quarterly numbers were on the line, closing contracts, even if it meant approving customizations, was the default decision at the leadership level. It was the norm through which the group consistently met their targets. The product team was trying to solve a leadership issue by building a process that likely wouldn't be followed. Sound familiar?

Issues with leadership behaviors and decision-making habits are often avoided because they require digging into less visible and deeply human problems with *individual mindsets* and *group dynamics*. People are more comfortable with neat and tidy processes and procedures than they are with messy people issues, so they focus on mechanizing the decision-making processes. Here's the thing: People are not only messy, they are also incredibly effective at finding ways to maintain their habits even within new systems. Organizational factors like processes and procedures are helpful, but done in isolation, they often come up short when it comes to inspiring behavior change across a group.

If you are leading a team, it is helpful to pay attention to how habits get reinforced within teams. Groups of people very quickly fall into norms that govern how they show up for each other, how they interact, and the ways in which they make decisions. Just think about any team you've been on for more than a minute. I'm guessing you've been on a team where status meetings are pretty routine. You go through the same agenda, sharing the same information, and you rehash the same decisions week after week. Even similar expressions are used across the team to refer to specific experiences, events, or challenges from the group's past, and the same stories are told by people as a means of representing how the group performs in different situations. You can shift things a little by adjusting factors like the structure of the agenda. But, understanding *HOW* to lead or work differently together requires putting in the effort to identify and name the group dynamics as well as the individual mindsets that drive the behaviors. From there, you can work to change them.

The Karrikins Behavior Model Basics

The most effective way to move your team through the Failure Gap and toward alignment is to create the space to talk about the influencers on the humans in your organization that are often left unspoken. Defining how to lead differently together depends on making those influencers visible, and therefore manageable. That's where the Behavior Model comes in. Created by Karrikins Group, this tool brings it all together in an easy-to-use model that helps to kick-start conversations about key influencers of decisions and behaviors that team members use to deliver outcomes. It's what drives completing your Diamond Triangle by defining *HOW* to lead together—the diamond of the triangle.

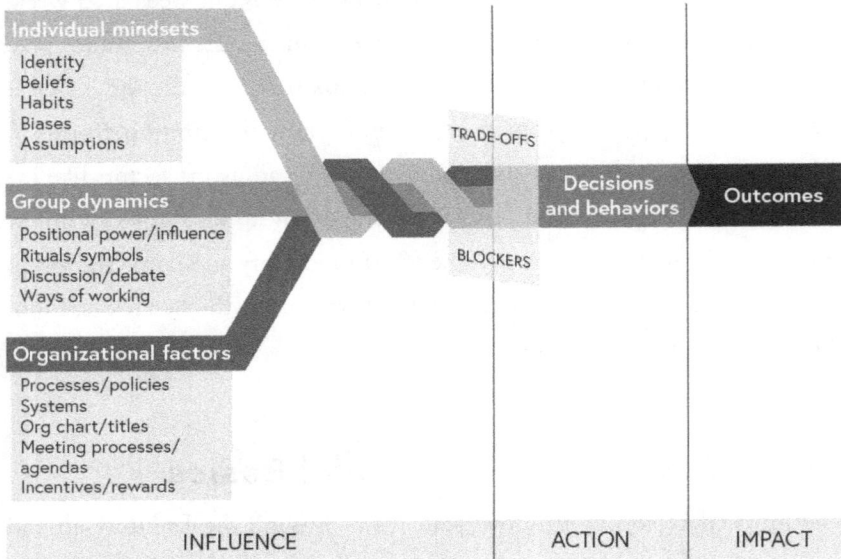

KARRIKINS® BEHAVIOR MODEL™

Broader context: regulatory, legal, industrial, geopolitical, environmental, ect.

Individual mindsets
- Identity
- Beliefs
- Habits
- Biases
- Assumptions

Group dynamics
- Positional power/influence
- Rituals/symbols
- Discussion/debate
- Ways of working

Organizational factors
- Processes/policies
- Systems
- Org chart/titles
- Meeting processes/agendas
- Incentives/rewards

TRADE-OFFS

BLOCKERS

Decisions and behaviors

Outcomes

INFLUENCE | ACTION | IMPACT

Image 4.2: Karrikins Behavior Model

When using this model, you can start on the left or the right to inspire new decisions and behaviors. Working from left to right, by identifying and giving voice to individual mindsets, group dynamics, and organizational factors, as well as trade-offs and blockers, you can start to see what is influencing the actions of decisions and behaviors. The impact of those actions are the outcomes that are created.

Working from right to left, if you know the new outcomes you need to deliver, you can identify the decisions and behaviors that leaders need to shift. From there, you can work back to the influencers (the individual mindsets, group dynamics, organizational factors, trade-offs, and blockers) that are in the way of those new actions.

The Behavior Model provides straightforward and accessible language for *solving the avoided*. Keep in mind that ambiguity protects the status quo. Removing ambiguity is the key to creating *aligned action* from leaders to deliver new outcomes for the business. It shows how outcomes are driven by decisions and behaviors that people engage in, intentionally or unintentionally. By working through the model, you make deeply habituated, and often invisible, leadership behaviors and decisions more accessible and manageable by bringing them forward in conversation. These behaviors and decisions might include things like not reallocating resources to support agreed-to priorities, sidelining specific colleagues, undoing decisions after the meeting via one-off conversations, always choosing short-term revenue over long-term investment, deciding to invest in operational consistency instead of innovation, and others.

Let's bring it together in a seemingly simple example. I'll never forget a client—I'll call her Mary—who was struggling to get her leadership team aligned on something as straightforward as setting the agenda for an off-site leadership event. Mary was the divisional president of a large consumer products company. She could have set the agenda herself and just told people what it was, but she decided to talk it through as a group and let the team determine how to best spend the time together. The WHAT was clear—set the meeting agenda. The WHY was clear too—make the best use of the time together. While it seemed like a simple thing to do, Mary learned otherwise.

> ### Ambiguity protects the status quo.

The first planning meeting for the off-site event was a disaster, and the team walked out with more questions than answers. Mary intentionally sat back and watched as the team tried to work through a decision-making process. A couple of very vocal members, Steve and Kristi, presented strong views on their need to have most of the time allocated to their areas. There was a fierce debate over the location, and the only thing they agreed on was to not decide where to go for dinner until a later meeting.

When Mary and I debriefed after the meeting, she acknowledged there were some well-established *group dynamics* that had played out.

Steve and Kristi, the two people who wanted to monopolize the time, were often seen as the most important people in the group because they ran sales teams in big geographies. She believed at least a few people in the room were disengaged because they had the *mindset* that, at the end of the day, the two louder people would be accommodated, so engaging wasn't useful or productive. The location choice was a hot topic because of the *trade-offs* it required from different team members. Some would have to put long trips onto already packed calendars and stretch already tight budgets to cover the costs.

Mary decided to get the team to try again, but with a slightly different setup, using the Behavior Model to facilitate an *intentional dialogue* approach to explore the *influencers*. She met with the individuals who seemed checked out and found that her instincts were right: They came with the assumption that their areas didn't matter as much and they didn't really have a voice. She also met with Steve and Kristi, who had the loudest voices in the room, and learned that they felt like they were doing the rest of the team a favor by taking the time to put together presentations and share what was going on with sales. She asked all of them to come to the next session ready to talk openly about the individual mindsets and group dynamics they were experiencing.

For the next planning meeting, Mary started off by asking people to share their perspectives on the value of meeting up in person and talk about the contribution they thought they could make. She wanted the whole team to hear from each member how they articulated these two things. After the team shared their thoughts, Mary asked people to share what surprised them about what they had heard. Here are a few nuggets from the conversation:

> » Steve and Kristi were surprised to learn that they were perceived
> as dominating the team's time together. They both shared that
> they assumed the team wanted to know all the details around

sales, and they thought they were being good "team players" by doing the work to provide so much background and information.

» The other members of the team were surprised to learn that Steve and Kristi were open to learning more about other parts of the business and working with them to make the sales and operations integration more effective.

» Everyone realized that they shared the challenge of packed calendars but that there were some unique hurdles for specific team members over the targeted week that it made sense to accommodate.

After spending some time making the influencers more visible, the team was able to work differently together to decide on an agenda and location that left everyone feeling heard, respected, and excited about getting together. They did not, however, manage to finalize dinner plans in that meeting! That came later, after a fierce debate over the merits of fancy tacos and Italian cuisine.

Mary's team went on to have a productive time together. More importantly, the experience helped the team have a better understanding of *HOW* they worked together to make decisions.

In Mary's case, in addition to getting to a decision about the off-site leadership event, she wanted to get her leaders working more as a team so they could tackle far more complex issues. By starting with something seemingly mundane and leveraging the Behavior Model as well as an intentional dialogue approach, she was able to make several important influencers visible and start shifting the team's decisions and behaviors in productive ways.

With this example in mind, let's take a deeper dive into the influencers of the Behavior Model.

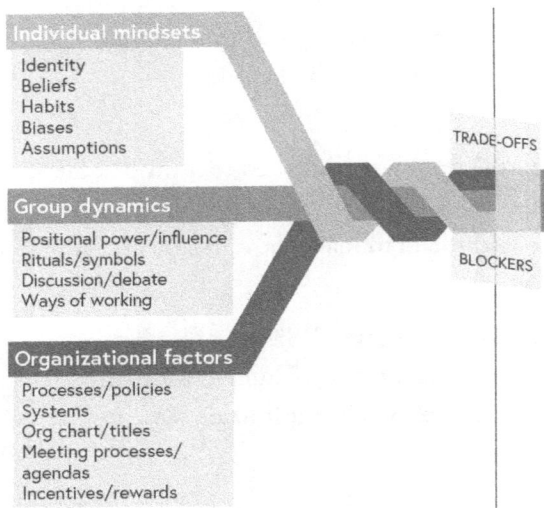

Individual mindsets

Identity
Beliefs
Habits
Biases
Assumptions

TRADE-OFFS

Group dynamics

Positional power/influence
Rituals/symbols
Discussion/debate
Ways of working

BLOCKERS

Organizational factors

Processes/policies
Systems
Org chart/titles
Meeting processes/
agendas
Incentives/rewards

Image 4.3: Focus on the Influencers of Behavior

Key Influencers

There are three key influencers on the left of the model that feed into secondary influencers:

1. **Individual mindsets** represent your deeply held beliefs, biases, and assumptions about other people, the ways work gets done, and how the world functions. Consider how you tend to respond to situations and what drives those responses. Think about the stories you tell yourself and others and what they reveal about how you default to showing up in certain situations in deeply habituated ways. When talking with your leadership team, you might hear common business mindsets like "I stay in my lane," "I need to deliver on my numbers first and foremost," "It isn't OK to fail or to miss a revenue target," or "I have to protect my team from the noise coming from other parts of the business."

2. **Group dynamics** exist whenever more than one person is in the room (physically or virtually). Everyone contributes to group dynamics, often in invisible ways. Groups create repeatable results

through things like rituals, symbols, default patterns, and power dynamics. Group dynamics may include "insider" language or acronyms, shared stories, the order in which people talk, the amount of airtime they are given, how decisions are made, and how tasks are assigned. They become deeply habituated across the team. Take some time to watch and note what happens on your team; you might be surprised by what you see.

3. **Organizational factors** create more visible guardrails for how things get done. They include things like defined processes, charts, rewards, salary bands, floor plans, parking assignments, working hours, and other structures that guide behaviors. Organizational factors might be beyond your control, but understanding the impact they have on you and your team is an important part of defining how to work together differently. A word of caution about organizational factors, though: Changing organizational factors is like changing gyms and wondering why you still aren't getting in shape. The location doesn't matter if you aren't working differently.

These three influencers combine to shape how people navigate the *trade-offs* and *blockers* they experience every day in their lives and in their work. But they aren't all equal. Many leaders default to thinking *organizational factors* are to blame for a lack of alignment. Organizational factors are certainly influencers that get in the way sometimes, but they are rarely the singular reason for something going wrong. Think about how often companies do a massive reorganization to try to fix something like breaking down silos, only to find that nothing really changes in the new structure. That's because *mindsets* and *group dynamics* didn't change, so people find ways to continue working the same way they always have, just through the new structure. It is important to dive deeply into mindsets and group dynamics while attending to organizational factors as you work through the Behavior Model to bring clarity and connection to how the influencers are contributing to outcomes.

Trade-Offs and Blockers

The influencers filter through the secondary influencers of *trade-offs* and *blockers* and ultimately determine the decisions and behaviors leaders act on. *Trade-offs* are things like short- and long-term investments. *Blockers* are obstacles like budget restrictions or regulatory requirements. By focusing on specific ways in which decisions and behaviors are influenced, teams and individuals change the outcomes they create by effectively changing the actions they take. Here are some of the most common trade-offs we hear:

Trade-offs

» Acting quickly/continuing analysis

» Operational consistency/innovation

» Long-term/short-term results

» Autonomy/collaboration

When teams stay in dialogue long enough to push past the obvious, we also hear about deeply personal trade-offs leaders feel they have to make. They start to give voice to the struggle to balance individual success, area success, and organizational success and the ways in which they feel pressured by group dynamics to go along with something before they've had a chance to voice their beliefs. We hear the stories that inform the default trade-offs—stories of executive purges and budgets being taken away, or of losing status or compensation because of a bet that went awry. We hear about the safe choices and the risky choices, and how people create boundaries around what they are willing to do. As we start to unpack all of this, it becomes obvious why so many leaders default to the safest possible trade-offs—protecting the status quo.

We all make trade-offs very quickly all the time—so quickly you might not even notice. Default reactions are strong, and you often can't see the deeper trade-off that sits behind a choice that's right in front of you. For me, when faced with a choice between pizza and salad, I'm obviously going for the pizza. But ultimately, that's trading long-term health for short-term gratification. If I can hit the pause button long enough to make that trade-off visible, there's a chance (however small) I'll make a different decision.

In business, a salesperson's decision to customize a product to win a customer might seem like a choice between winning or losing an important contract, with the obvious answer being to close the deal. But it might also be a trade-off between the short-term revenue and the long-term cost to serve that customer, resulting in a low-margin customer relationship. Building the muscle to have deeper conversations about the less obvious trade-off or a trade-off that is often avoided is where the hard work gets done to align to shared goals.

Here's another example—a team member comes to a leader with a bold new idea for changing an operational process that everyone knows is broken, but the team also knows how to work around it. The leader says no to the new idea because it might cause a disruption that would result in the team missing important metrics. The leader may believe they are making a sound decision to reduce risk, avoid costs, and manage any potential fallout. A less comfortable reality may be that they are also trading innovation for short-term predictability, which may create more risk for the operations of the business in the future. Going even deeper, they may be unwilling to risk the security of knowing they can make their numbers in the broken system because of the potential for reputational damage as a leader if the new idea fails.

Trade-offs never go away—you are always negotiating choices that must be made, and there are rarely right or wrong answers. As in the previous example, protecting reliable operations is a reasonable goal for a manager to have. And problems arise when squelching innovation becomes the default response instead of a carefully weighed decision based on whether there is an opportunity to take on some risk and try something new. Defaulting to the protectionist position may seem reasonable, but it will ultimately drive employee disengagement and result in the business lagging behind more innovative competitors.

Digging to get beyond the obvious default choice and into the trade-off being made gives teams the opportunity to work differently together when those moments come up. And they come up every day. What are some of the trade-offs you and your team are making that hold you back or move you forward? Take a moment and list them here or elsewhere, then have a conversation with your team to get their thoughts too.

» _____

» _____

» _____

» _____

» _____

Blockers are similar to trade-offs, but they feel like less of a choice. They may be a centrally mandated requirement or a board-level direction. They may also be practical, like working across time zones or in different languages. Blockers include things like:

» Organizational structures

» Mandated metrics

» Budget allocations

» Hiring restrictions

- » Conflicting goals

- » Talent gap/hiring restrictions

Whether something is cataloged by you and your team as a trade-off or a blocker is up to you—there is no right or wrong answer. It has to do with context, levels of authority, span of control, and personal belief structures, so what appears to one person as a trade-off might be a blocker to another. Don't worry too much about how you inventory something. Instead, pay more attention to making it visible and talking with your team about how they react when it comes up.

These often-invisible influencers affect how you respond to trade-offs and blockers, which ultimately drives your decisions and behaviors as a leader. The result? Missed opportunities as competitors pass you by or customers move on, or risks like disenchanted and frustrated employees.

Keep in mind that small shifts in your influencers can have big impacts on the outcomes you create. Shifts in your key influencers change how you orient toward trade-offs and blockers and by extension change the decisions you ultimately make that drive outcomes.

Default responses to influencers drive business-as-usual outcomes.

For a more targeted situation you have with your team or company, you can use our Making the Invisible Visible worksheet to have a conversation with your team about their experiences.

When using this worksheet, start by thinking about a specific scenario. Maybe it is your annual strategy cycle, budgeting, or QBRs. Perhaps it is a transformation you have in progress or a big strategic goal. Or it could be smaller—like planning a leadership event or doing effective code reviews on a development team. Whatever the situation, think about the things that are often left unsaid and make a note of them. You should also take the time to spot the things the team does well—the strengths you want to amplify. Then get very specific about the key influencers of mindsets, group dynamics, and organizational factors as well as trade-offs and blockers that are getting in the way.

Making the invisible visible is all about how you create the space for those conversations to happen. Ask your colleagues to add to the list—what would they like to explore as a team? Don't hesitate to write your thoughts below, type them up elsewhere, or download the worksheet as you answer these questions:

MAKING THE INVISIBLE VISIBLE

Use the Karrikins Group Behavior Model to consider questions that help uncover the specific, visible behavior changes needed to move from agreement to alignment.

Topic or issue:

What are 1 to 3 things that go unspoken or are avoided?	What are 1 to 3 mindsets that get in the way (biases, assumptions, beliefs, etc.)?	What are the biggest trade-offs that are a struggle to navigate?
What are 1 to 3 things we do well in this space?	What are 1 to 3 examples of suboptimal group dynamics (discussion, debate, ways of working, etc.)?	What are the main blockers that slow us down?

What are 1 to 3 organizational factors that get in the way
(processes, compensation, systems, structures, etc.)?

Image 4.4: Making the Invisible Visible Worksheet

It is crucial to talk with your colleagues for their input—conversation is where behavior shifts start to happen. For right now, just focus with them on identifying the influencers. Later on, we will talk about shifting into new decisions and behaviors. When we do this work with teams, we spend the majority of our time in these conversations about influencers and trade-offs. They are often challenging, but when teams lean in and do the work, they change the trajectory of their outcomes and the ways in which the team needs to shift how they are behaving. The decisions they are making become very obvious.

It can be productive to do this, and it can also be confronting. It brings up deeply held, and often invisible, influencers of our behaviors that might not be easy to talk about. But if you don't create clarity around and connection to the key influencers, trade-offs, and blockers, you won't be able to commit to the decisions and behaviors that drive new outcomes.

Action and Impact

As the influencers come together and move into trade-offs and blockers, action happens through *decisions and behaviors* that drive *outcomes*. In simple terms, decisions and behaviors are things like putting investment dollars toward innovative new products or showing up with a curious approach to solving a problem. Examples include leaders who reallocate budget, change metrics, or ask great questions. Outcomes are what you deliver. Examples of positive outcomes include successfully transforming your organization, adopting new technology, changing your go-to-market approach, or having a productive off-site leadership event. These actions should be aligned in support of larger goals and commitments (the WHAT and the WHY), but they are often misaligned because of conditioned responses to trade-offs and blockers, driven by the habituated influencers that drive negative outcomes like missed transformation goals, lack of progress on programs or strategies, and outdated ways of working together. We are going to work more on changing decisions and behaviors in the next section.

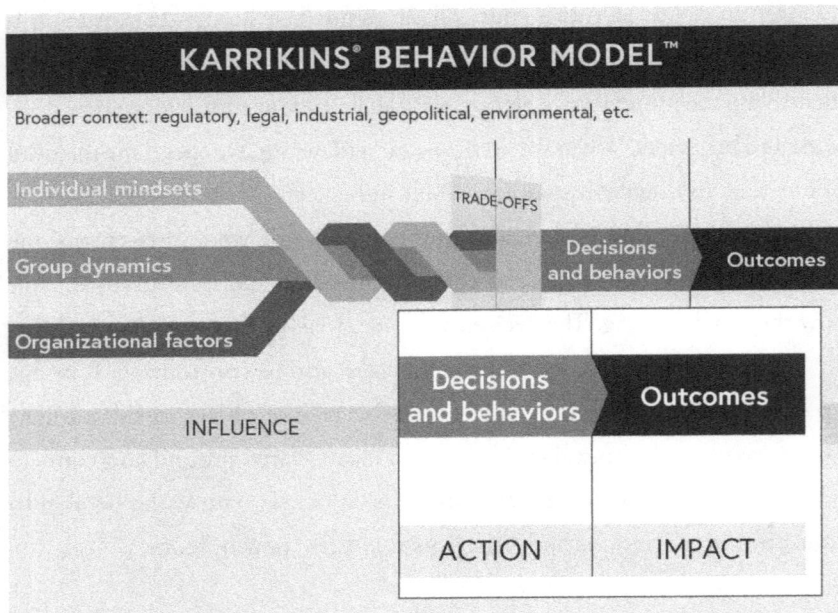

Image 4.5: Focus on Decisions, Behaviors, and Outcomes

People are not objective decision-makers, despite what they might believe.

Working through the Behavior Model helps shake an individual or team out of conditioned ways of working by making these often-invisible influencers visible and creating the space for new dialogue. By talking together, teams can start to shift the deeply habituated responses they have both individually and collectively. We call this "creating clarity and connection." Giving voice to the invisible influencers and openly grappling with the trade-offs and blockers fuels the ability to commit to different behaviors and decisions and to have the courage to stick with it when trade-offs are tough to make. This is the path to delivering new, and often transformative, outcomes.

Stories Help Make the Invisible Visible

It takes courage to work through what's getting in the way of new team behaviors and decisions. Finding the space to shine a light on these influencers can be difficult to do directly, so we often ask people to share stories—examples of where the group or individuals are making choices that leave the team stuck in agreement that something is a good idea. We hear so many of those stories when we work with teams, and those can be gold mines of information about how a team works (or doesn't work) together.

Consider your own team or one you've been on in the past and the examples used to represent what your team does well and not well. You probably hear (or tell) the same stories over and over. Often these are "hero stories" about the development team that worked through the night to meet a deadline, or the salespeople who worked nonstop to hit their quarterly goals, or the executive who drove through the night to deliver a product to a customer. If you want to change the hero mentality and move into a culture where you avoid fires instead of fighting them, you have to identify those stories and stop telling them, because they reinforce the habit of playing the hero for people on the team and in the broader group.

In the early 2000s I worked with a client who manufactured fairly specialized electronics. They needed to overhaul their distribution system, which was primarily through a large network of specialty stores throughout the United States. Competitors on Amazon were starting to take market share, and they had a choice to make: Either partner with Amazon or try to build their own digital shopping experience to give customers the opportunity to shop online.

As we talked through the need to think differently about distribution, there were several mindsets and group dynamics that came up, and the team consistently used the same examples to reinforce the validity of their beliefs and behaviors. For example, they were convinced their customers would not use Amazon to purchase their specialty products. They had a favorite story about a customer that they used to reinforce this belief. A customer had told a salesperson that there was no way he'd ever consider buying these types of products online. This was a very well-respected customer, who had been with them a long time, and many of the senior leadership team members knew him personally. As soon as someone brought that example up, everyone would nod and say they remembered that. You could feel them relax, because now there was a reason not to solve this very difficult problem. This small story played a powerful role in reinforcing a group dynamic that held the leadership team back from taking on the work they most needed to: dealing with the biggest threat to their business, which was the rise of online shopping. But this customer story, together with a few others that were frequently retold, reinforced that business as usual was OK. Sometimes it is hard to believe the power of stories to drive results, but when a group is so deeply grounded in this type of defining story, it can be extremely difficult to break free of the narrative and get to what's behind the decisions and behaviors at a leadership level.

People often also avoid talking specifically about individual mindsets and group dynamics because it can be uncomfortable. It requires speaking about things that are culturally normed to be invisible. That might show up when a more tenured team member reinforces the status quo by referencing historical examples, and less tenured team members are reluctant to suggest it might be time to retire that example and look at the situation from a current perspective. Another place this shows up is when people hesitate to speak clearly about how a strategic decision will have a negative impact on one part of the business while positively impacting another. The result is that a strategic priority gets sidelined because no one wants to tackle the elephant in the room, which is that part of the business will take a hit and might become obsolete.

Mining Organizational Stories

In 2010, I was working with a very large financial services company. Many companies in that industry were doing massive digital transformations at the time. Interacting with customers on smart devices like iPhones was just starting to be allowed by regulatory agencies and accepted by customers, and everyone was playing catch-up with their technologies.

At the company I worked with, there was a persistent belief that the employees were not very good at technology implementations. Several failed experiences in the past had lead to all sorts of stories that they would tell as we prepared to support the change-management effort associated with the new technology. There was a pervasive "this too shall pass" energy among the people who most needed to be energetically engaged. As we worked to figure out what was going on, we started asking people to tell us stories about past efforts to upgrade this technology.

What was fascinating to me was how many people talked about one specific effort called Omega. The Omega program had been a technology upgrade effort that had run from the late 1990s to the early 2000s—so over a decade prior to our work. It failed miserably, the company took a huge write-off, and quite a few people associated with the program lost their jobs. Despite so much time passing, the story of Omega was told over and over when people reflected on the challenges of implementing new technologies. In fact, some of the people who told the Omega story weren't even with the company when it happened!

That's how deeply stories imprint on groups and influence beliefs and behaviors. They get replicated across generations of employees until they become corporate lore. This particular story was shaping the way people oriented toward any effort to upgrade mission-critical systems. Their decisions about allocating resources, setting priorities, and engaging with the upgrade effort were heavily influenced by beliefs and mindsets that were reinforced by stories like the one about Omega. The clear message was that it wouldn't work, the company would step back before it was completed, and people who got too close were either wasting their time or would get fired. With everyone walking around with that as their context, it was no surprise the efforts failed again and again.

The power of stories to establish context and beliefs also happens among families and friends. I suspect you know a family story you've heard so many times you can tell it as if you were there—only you weren't. Or maybe you just weren't at an age where you could reasonably remember it. In the retelling of it, you reinforce group norms and communicate values while signaling your membership. This is part of how oral history works to build community, and the same thing happens at work. It isn't a bad thing—the people who participate in it aren't lying; they are engaging in very human behavior to help make sense of how they exist within a structure around them.

By bringing these types of narratives to the forefront, teams can start to orient differently toward them. In the case of Omega, one of the ways we worked to activate leaders to energetically drive the transformation was by getting them to start dealing with the lore head-on by sharing with their teams how the new effort was distinctly different and how they were going to lead differently to successfully transform. Every time Omega was brought up, leaders very intentionally shifted the dialogue to the future and the outcomes they were working toward. By consistently changing the focus of the conversation and drawing clear distinctions, over time leaders were able to get their people to finally stop retelling the Omega story. In fact, they had an official retirement party to put it to rest, and they used that opportunity to start telling new stories about the small successes they were having with the current work.

Note they didn't try to rewrite history. Omega was a huge failure, with a lot of fallout. There was no changing that reality, and leaders acknowledged that rather than trying to deny it. But the leaders changed how they were leading by consistently redirecting the conversation when Omega came up, reframing and creating new anchors until Omega was no longer the defining story for the organization.

There are three takeaways I want you to keep in mind from this example:

1. Identifying the impact of stories like Omega is useful in understanding why teams stay stuck in agreement without taking action to align and deliver together.

2. When you hear a story like this, you can't change it or deny it, but you can reframe its impact on the culture and the belief structures in the organization.

3. Dealing with a story like this doesn't happen in one declaration along the lines of "Thou shalt not tell this story anymore." It happens gradually, as leaders change themselves by consistently reflecting, redirecting, and reframing the story instead of allowing it to be an anchor. It takes small, consistent actions over time to create change.

Identifying stories like Omega can help make visible the deeply held mindsets, assumptions, beliefs, and biases that people bring into transformation efforts. It also helps show us more about group dynamics, including the context the group works within, the influence of positional power, symbols of membership, and decision-making norms. All of these have an impact on the ways of working together that influence how a team manages opportunities and risks.

Cataloging stories that have a big impact on your company's transformation is a great way to bring clarity and connection to them. Our Story Capture worksheet is an easy way to start the process by having a conversation with your colleagues about the stories they hear and tell.

STORY CAPTURE WORKSHEET

Use the Story Capture worksheet to identify the stories you and your colleagues use to explain "how things work around here" or even how they *don't* work! These include common examples people cite, big moments people remember, or client stories that help people make sense of decisions.

What are the highlights of the story?

-
-
-
-

When does it get told?	What does it explain to people?

What's a good name for this story?

Naming the story helps you to spot it faster when it comes up and gives you a way to shift the story in a new direction if necessary.

Image 4.1: Story Capture Worksheet

What stories are you hearing that might give you clues about the influencers on people's decisions and behaviors? Ask your colleagues as well—what stories do they hear over and over that help them understand the organization? Once you identify a story, give it a name to make it easy to recognize going forward. You'll be amazed at how often the same stories pop up once you start naming them. Stories are one of the ways behaviors are fueled and norms are reinforced, and making them visible gives you the opportunity to work with them in new ways that change the direction of your organization.

Putting the Behavior Model to Work

Let's go back to Sara's TT1 for a moment. They agreed they should collaborate more, but they just weren't doing it. Over time, they missed opportunities and risks because they weren't connecting with one another effectively. In crucial moments, they typically decided to go it alone rather than engaging one another in collaborative opportunities. Their deeply held mindsets and group dynamics meant that when they encountered a trade-off or a blocker to collaborating, they decided to work independently in spite of their agreement that collaboration was a good idea.

They would periodically focus on collaboration and promise to do better going forward (side note—raise your hand if you've ever done that with a goal to have a healthier diet or work out more). They'd created some goals around it, most of which went by the wayside or were half-heartedly met. They even included "collaboration" in their values statements as a reminder of how important they thought it was. They periodically engaged in catalytic events designed to spark collaboration in a big way but quickly reverted back to business as usual within a few days of the event.

They had addressed some of the organizational factors getting in the way of collaboration, but they hadn't dug into what was influencing them in the moment when they had to decide whether they would collaborate or not. Something was getting in the way of deciding to reach out to their peers and get input, support, ideas, and cautions as they built solutions for their own areas.

This is an incredibly common scenario in the workplace. There's an agreement that things should be different, but also a lack of clarity about and connection to the idea that drives commitment to it when faced with trade-offs or blockers.

Let's take a look at how Sara's team might break down the Behavior Model from right to left using *collaboration* as an example:

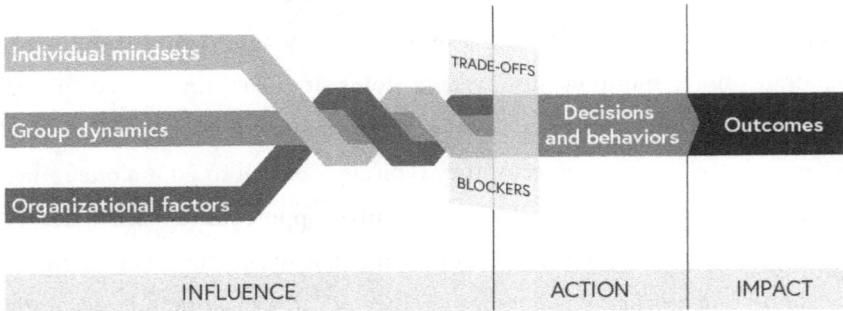

KARRIKINS® BEHAVIOR MODEL™

Broader context: regulatory, legal, industrial, geopolitical, environmental, etc.

Individual mindsets

Group dynamics

Organizational factors

TRADE-OFFS

BLOCKERS

Decisions and behaviors

Outcomes

INFLUENCE | ACTION | IMPACT

Image 4.6: Karrikins Behavior Model

» **Desired outcome:** More cross-team collaboration drives better results.

» **Desired decisions and behaviors:** Include other people in ideation and problem-solving; be open to input from others; leverage the knowledge and capabilities of the whole group more effectively.

» **Trade-off:** Move quickly and autonomously or slow down and bring others in.

» **Blocker:** Time zones are hard to navigate, so collaborating in real time is a challenge.

» **Current individual mindset:** Collaboration takes a long time and doesn't add much value—it's a nice-to-have, not a must-have.

» **Current group dynamics:** Our group treats asking for help or input as a sign of weakness, and they try to take over the decision.

» **Current organizational factors:** My team's success is pegged to metrics that run counter to collaboration, like our speed to market, time to resolution, etc.

By digging deeper into the question of what gets in the way of collaboration, Sara's team realized there were deeply held beliefs that the collaboration equation didn't add up—that it took too much time and effort relative to the improved outcomes it provided. Another challenge that was identified through this conversation was that *collaborate* wasn't consistently defined. Some people saw it as asking someone casually in the hallway about a problem they were having, while others saw it as requiring large-scale events to bring big groups together to workshop a specific situation.

The conversations spurred by the Behavior Model made it clear that the team team didn't need another catalytic event or a new collaboration process (although those have a time and place); they needed to be honest with one another about what they thought collaboration meant and the impact they felt it would have on the outcomes they were trying to create.

CASE STUDY

At SnackInvasion, Jordon and Sandy also pulled their leadership team together. They carved out the time to discuss what they had to do to change individually and as a team to succeed with the ERP transformation, which was a large, multiyear, complex technology program. They knew their senior leaders needed to stay engaged with the work well beyond the kick-off, and they needed to start thinking differently about what it meant to successfully lead their regions through this difficult time.

When they broke down the Behavior Model from right to left from a perspective of *transformation*, they discovered the following:

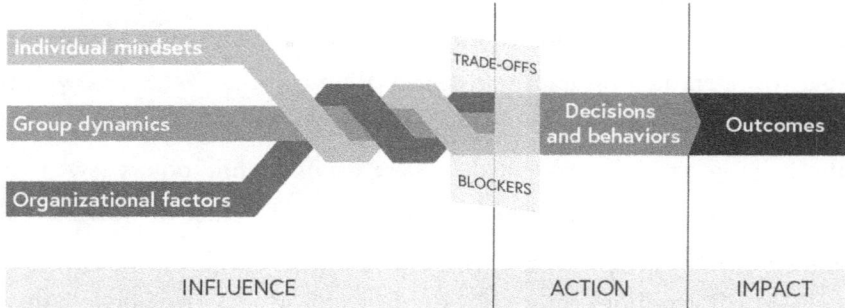

Image 4.6: Karrikins Behavior Model

- » **Desired outcome:** A successful ERP consolidation would reduce costs and increase effectiveness while helping them to better serve customers and making it easier to share internal resources across geographies.

- » **Desired decisions and behaviors:** Senior leaders would activate their own leadership by making decisions that supported their region standardizing. They would behave in ways that were consistent with the end goal of working from one system. When they would hear noise from their people about the level of effort and the difficulties, leaders would focus on solving for the future state rather than giving in to maintaining the current state. Area presidents would develop a fluent understanding of the future state platform and start using that language to talk with their people, emphasizing taking the time to do things differently rather than pushing for things to be done quickly.

- » **Trade-off:** Work harder and take more time to get to standard processes or customize for regional preferences to get the work done faster.

» **Blocker:** Local markets with specific legal and regulatory needs have to be managed while moving toward more standard processes.

» **Current individual mindset:** I want to protect my people from having to do extra work, and I have to protect my reputation as always delivering on my quarterly goals. I want to reduce the "noise" this transformation is causing for my people.

» **Current group dynamics:** Each region does what is best for them so they can make their numbers, and no one wants to be the leader whose region comes up short. There is a lot of peer pressure around quarterly numbers, and they don't have time to pay attention to what's happening in other regions.

» **Current organizational factors:** Executive bonuses are tied to quarterly results, so missing a number because people have been working on the transformation effort has a material impact.

You can use the Behavior Model to help your team come together and align to take action on what you need to do. Start with the outcomes (WHAT) you are working toward, and work backward through the new behaviors, decisions, and influencers of those actions. Give it a try here!

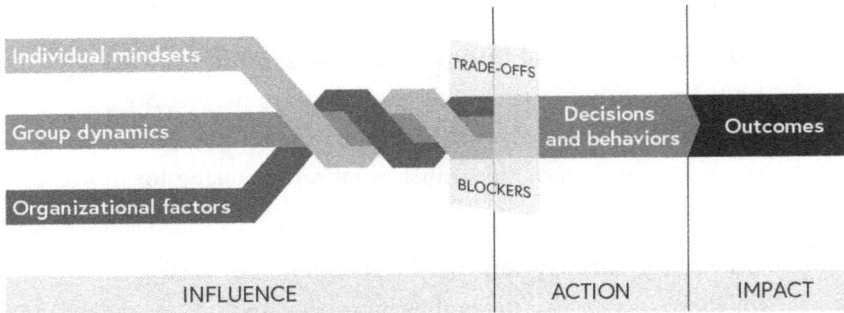

KARRIKINS® BEHAVIOR MODEL™

Broader context: regulatory, legal, industrial, geopolitical, environmental, etc.

Individual mindsets

Group dynamics

Organizational factors

TRADE-OFFS

Decisions and behaviors

Outcomes

BLOCKERS

INFLUENCE   ACTION   IMPACT

Image 4.6: Karrikins Behavior Model

» **Desired outcome:**

_____

» **Desired decisions and behaviors:**

_____

» **Trade-offs:**

_____

» **Blockers:**

_____

» **Current individual mindset:**

_____

» **Current group dynamics:**

_____

» **Current organizational factors:**

_____

To align a team to shared goals, you need to host conversations with your team about each of the influencers and actions in the Behavior Model that lead to the outcomes you are working toward. By working back through the model to understand the necessary intentional shifts in individual mindsets, group dynamics, organizational factors, trade-offs, and blockers, you create the conditions for new behaviors and decisions to happen.

I know I keep repeating this, but it is so important to remember that working through the Behavior Model takes time and energy from the team doing the work. While it can be very helpful to have a third party host the conversation so the whole team participates appropriately, you can't out-source or delegate the discussions—you and your colleagues need to be in them. It is through the time spent in discussion that people make sense of the shifts that need to happen and mutually negotiate what a different way of working looks like.

I find this is especially challenging when I work with senior executives, although it applies to teams at any level. If you and your team need to work differently together, you have to figure that out for yourselves—you can't get someone else to do it for you. And that means grappling with your personal mindsets and group dynamics and the habituated ways you navigate trade-offs, blockers, changing behaviors, and decision-making to drive new outcomes. Just like a therapist can ask you the right questions but can't tell you the right answers, a good alignment facilitator can make sure you are in the right conversations and that the pace, content, and participation are well managed, but they can't give the team the answer to how to lead better together.

> At Karrikins Group, we've said no to working with teams who aren't willing to commit to doing the work to *make HOW matter*. It isn't worth the investment of our time and their resources to work with a team who just wants to be told the answer.

Nudges, Not Shoves

When I work with teams on alignment, I encourage them to think about *nudges, not shoves.* That means finding the small things that can *shift* mindsets and group dynamics, as well as trade-offs and blockers, effectively and consistently over time rather than trying to make massive behavior changes across a group of people. It is hard enough for one person to change—let alone a team of people. Don't set yourself up for failure by trying to tackle big leaps. Focus on small shifts you can consistently deliver on over time.

Shifts represent nudges that redirect decisions and behaviors when trade-offs and blockers come up. They tie back to mindsets, group dynamics, and also organizational factors and are ways of making visible the small but powerful changes that, done consistently, drive new outcomes. Discovering effective shifts starts with identifying the mindsets and group dynamics that are misaligned with the desired outcome and then cataloging the trade-offs and blockers that the team experiences.

CASE STUDY

Sara's TT1 got together and started a dialogue about collaboration and what it meant to each of them. They carved out two hours every other week for ten weeks to identify and build a shared understanding of what they needed to shift individually and collectively. In those discussions, they explored mindsets and group dynamics and created a checklist of organizational factors they experienced as barriers. They also started to notice and name situations where they felt like they were caught in a trade-off related to collaboration. They came up with a list of shifts that would support collaboration, including:

> » **Individual mindsets** could shift from *Collaboration takes too long* (starting point) to *Investing in collaboration will*

speed things up later when we need to move fast together (shift). Another old mindset was *Collaboration is a nice-to-have, not a must-have* (starting point). This was changed to *Just because I can do it alone doesn't mean I should do it alone* (shift).

» **Group dynamics** needed to change from *We stay in our lanes out of respect for one another* (starting point) to *It's OK to ask questions and offer suggestions* (shift). As a group, they made the time for that to happen. They went from *We must be efficient in our time together so we get back to our real jobs* (starting point) to *Working together as a team is also part of our "real jobs"* (shift).

» **Organizational factors** weren't something the team could always fix, but they could acknowledge them and make them visible, allowing the team to work differently. They realized that *Working across time zones wasn't impossible* (shift). With the right platform, they could collaborate with people in other time zones.

» **Trade-offs and blockers** were mostly around time and the lack of it. They came up with a nickname for when they were in the trade-off of wanting to move quickly or bringing others in—they called it the Time Warp. When they were in the situation, someone would say, "Hey, are we in the Time Warp on this?" and this was a signal to the rest of the team that they needed to stop and think about how they were working and if it was a moment to start collaborating. It is such a small thing, but it has such a huge impact when teams develop this kind of shared language. It sends a signal to pause and re-evaluate the default course of action.

Sara and her team understood these kinds of shifts weren't giant leaps; they were *nudges* meant to break the cycle of default thinking and help individuals and the group start to work differently together. Note that the organizational factor shift didn't include fixing the blocker of time zones—there's no way to alter time and space—but naming it and shifting what it means to collaborate opened up some space to work across time zones more effectively. Sometimes you have control over organizational factors—though many times you don't—but there is value in making sure everyone understands and appreciates the challenge so you can work differently together as you work through them. When you've taken the time to talk through the influencers and make them visible and consistently make small shifts in how you are showing up, it is amazing how fast you can progress toward new ways of working together.

By identifying the current influencers you need to shift, you can work with them differently to create new decision and behavior patterns when the inevitable trade-offs and blockers come up. By shifting even a little bit, you create new outcomes. Take a look at our Shifts worksheet, and think about how you might create even small shifts in influencers that would have a big impact on outcomes.

Are there small things that have become visible to you as you've been working through this book that might be helpful to start moving into action? Take a few minutes to jot down some shifts you see for yourself in how you lead or work with your team and have a conversation with your colleagues about the shifts that can be made by all team members.

PERSONALIZED SHIFTS WORKSHEET

Use this worksheet to identify a few shifts you'd like to track for yourself. Over the next few weeks, check in periodically and rank yourself, to see if you are making progress. Just the step of checking in will help you build momentum.

Individual Mindsets		Group Dynamics	
How might you shift your mindset about working together?		How could you contribute to a new group dynamic to help your team align?	
FROM	TO	FROM	TO

Organizational Factors you are working to shift:

FROM [ ] TO [ ]

Image 4.7: Personalized Shifts Worksheet

Never lose sight of this being about nudges, not shoves. It is important not to attempt this work with a "big bang" approach. People need time and space to think through what they've heard and shared and to synthesize the information in new ways. The biggest mistake I see with highly action-oriented teams is the desire to just "get it done" and slap some good words on a page instead of slowing down and genuinely creating shared meaning through dialogue. It never works, because people are not machines. They can't just be programmed once and expected to repeat the same motions over and over. It takes meaningful and intentional practice over time to change how you work together.

Here are a few questions to get the conversation moving with your leadership team about shifts you can make together. Ultimately, these questions ladder up to answering the bigger question of: How do we need to lead differently to get different results? Getting them dialed in will help you have intentional dialogue about creating new outcomes.

We'll use collaboration as an example, since many teams struggle with collaboration, but you could replace it with whatever you are working on with your team. For example, the SnackInvasion team might replace *collaboration* with *transformation*.

» How do I define collaboration, and how does my definition compare with others?

» What do I believe is the hypothetical, but not real, value of collaboration?

» What are the stories I tell myself about collaboration (good and bad)?

» How would collaborating impact my colleagues across the organization?

» What do we tend to trade collaboration for in our day-to-day jobs?

These are examples related to aligning on the goal of getting aligned to better collaboration. How else could you explore the influencers that are holding back alignment in your scenario through asking questions that make the influencers visible? Use the Intentional Dialogue worksheet to help you identify influencers and discover shifts that would be helpful as you go forward.

By identifying the mindsets, group dynamics, and organizational factors you need to shift and how they impact trade-offs and blockers, you can work with them differently and create new decision and behavior patterns when the inevitable trade-offs and blockers come up. By shifting even a little bit, you create new outcomes.

Of course, these are fairly surface-level examples of how to use the Behavior Model, but I'm confident you can take the approach outlined in the worksheets and apply it to many situations where you find there is agreement but not alignment. When we work with teams, we go much deeper into how to strengthen the team's muscles to work differently together when inevitable challenges come up. Teams can learn to identify influencers quickly and to create the shifts they need to make to drive new decisions and behaviors. When teams learn how to do this, they start to build the capability to get aligned and deliver together on anything they need to tackle as a team.

Shared language, understanding, and meaning that come through dialogue create the small but powerful nudges that change the trajectory of a team's outcomes. In some cases, it can mean the difference between a failed business and a successful legacy. Shifting the conversations you are having might seem obvious, but it is very difficult to implement. In the next section, we are going to talk about how to take the shifts you've identified and put them into practice through new ways of working together.

KEY TAKEAWAYS

- » Teams can fall into deeply habituated ways of working that can cause them to get stuck in the Failure Gap.

- » The stories you and your team members tell are powerful motivators for behaviors and can indicate how the team is working together (or not) and why.

- » The key influencers of individual mindsets, group dynamics, and organizational factors play a significant role in how you deliver outcomes.

» The key influencers come together to drive the secondary influencers of trade-offs and blockers that everyone, including you, experience.

» Typically, there are no "right" answers for trade-offs; you have to negotiate them in every situation. The important thing is to do that intentionally instead of habitually.

» Blockers often can't be solved, but you can change the conversations you are having about them so you can deal with them more directly.

» When you have open and honest conversations about the key influencers and secondary influencers, you start to shift from agreement to alignment.

» Shifts are incredibly powerful tools for changing behaviors and decisions and ultimately driving new outcomes. Shifts should be nudges not shoves—they are best as small things done consistently over time.

Check out www.makehowmatter.com/worksheets
for more resources.

If you aren't transforming how you lead, you aren't transforming your organization.

5

New Ways of Working:
P-HOWS Make the Difference

If you spend too much time thinking about a thing, you'll never get it done. Make at least one definite move daily toward your goal.

—Bruce Lee, martial artist and actor

ALIGNING TO NEW WAYS OF working as colleagues, leaders, peers, and teammates starts with making influencers visible and understanding them in new ways. By doing the work to shine a light on the influencers you and your colleagues experience, you can notice and name them. This provides a path to responding differently when they come up. As you move to making decisions individually and as a team, you can use this new language to drive different conversations, which fuels the shifts in the influencers that drive new behaviors and decisions that then drive different outcomes.

When I see teams struggle to deliver new outcomes despite knowing WHAT they need to do differently and WHY, most of the time, they haven't done the work as a team to get clear on their influencers. They jump ahead to the new behaviors and decisions they need, but they don't have the foundation required to deal with real-life situations that keep them in their deeply habituated responses. If you've had the conversations we talked about in the previous chapters and built clarity about and connection to the influencers, committing to new ways of working becomes exponentially easier.

Check It Out for Yourself

Jumping ahead to action plays out in my personal life as well. If I want to get to a different outcome, I fixate on the behaviors I need to change without unpacking the personal equivalents of mindsets, group dynamics, organizational factors, trade-offs, and blockers. Because I haven't sorted out how to shift my influencers, I end up trying to muscle through behavior change because I know WHAT I need to do differently, but I don't know HOW to be different in the important moments.

Does that ever happen to you? Remember, most New Year's resolutions fail, so it happens to a lot of people!

Here's how it happens for me. Let's say I'm going on vacation to Argentina next year. I decide I want to do something ambitious, like learn Spanish in time for the trip—I have a year, after all! I know WHAT I need to do—consistently study, practice, and learn over time. I know WHY I want to do it—to make traveling even more fun by having some command of the local language and culture. So, I focus on the *behaviors* and *decisions* I need to change, and I break down what I need to do into six steps in ninety-day sprints. It is a beautiful project plan, and it looks something like this:

1. Download a language app to my phone, sign up, and pay the annual fee.

2. Schedule thirty minutes a day to progress through lessons.

3. In ninety days (~2,700 minutes into my lessons), start attending a local language club to practice.

4. Attend the club once a week for ninety days.

5. For the third ninety-day segment, through the club, find a tutor to work with me to fine-tune my now well-developed language skills.

6. In the last three months before my departure date, speak in Spanish (with a perfect Argentinian accent) at least thirty minutes a day with my new besties from the club (who are amazed at my command of the language).

Here's how it actually plays out:

1. Download the app, sign up, and pay the annual fee.

2. Open the first lesson and move through it quickly thanks to some high school Spanish; end feeling great.

3. Decide to do the first five lessons in the first day because I'm doing awesome.

4. Skip days 2 to 4 because I'm already ahead and I have some wiggle room.

5. Forget to do lessons days 6 through 10, and now I'm behind.

6. Day 11, do another five lessons to try to catch up.

7. Day 12 through 365, see the lesson reminder on my calendar and think *I can catch up tomorrow.*

8. Day 365, download a translation app and resolve to rely on the kindness of locals on my trip.

9. Day 366, realize I forgot to cancel the auto-renewal and accidentally paid for a second year of Spanish lessons I'll never use.

Does that sound familiar? Here's where I went wrong: I tried to build in new behaviors and make different decisions about what to do with my time without getting honest with myself about the mindsets, social context, and environmental factors (personal versions of our team-based influencers) that fuel my decisions and behaviors. So, I was left to try to power through behavior change without the support of clearly articulated shifts in *influencers* that I could use to guide new actions. I didn't have the clarity and connection I needed to commit to new decisions and behaviors. Imagine if I had taken the time up front to notice and name some of them: The WHAT and the WHY would have remained the same. And the *HOW* might have sounded something like this:

» **Individual mindset** changed from *I can do these lessons fast and just catch up if I fall behind* (starting point) to *The human brain (and therefore my brain) works better in small doses absorbed consistently, so building a habit around a few minutes a day is more effective than episodic binging to learn a new language* (shift).

» **Group dynamics** (social context) changed from *I don't want to tell anyone what I'm doing because it might be embarrassing if I fail* (starting point) to *I have a good friend from Argentina who I could ask to help me by reviewing my lessons each week and working with me to fine-tune things* (shift).

» **Organizational factors** (environmental factors) went from *I already have so much to do every day, there's no way to fit it in* (starting point) to *I could replace twenty minutes of online scrolling over lunch to make it happen* (shift).

I should have known my WHAT and my WHY were insufficient to create sustained behavior change—I do this for a living! But you know how that goes. I needed to think about *HOW* I was going to show up differently to get where I wanted to go—to learn Spanish before my trip. And yet . . . I never did utter a word of Spanish in a perfect Argentinian accent, because I tried to change what I was doing without activating new ways of approaching my desired outcome, which was to learn Spanish.

Leader Activation—Asking the Right Questions

We talked earlier about the difference between leader activation and change management. Recall that leader activation is about how you *lead* differently; change management is about what you *do* differently. I make that distinction because if there's one thing I've observed in working with all sorts of teams and leaders during times of transformation, it's that *leaders love to change other people, but they don't love changing themselves.* All too often, especially during times of massive transformation, change is left up to the "doers" in the organization—the people with their boots on the ground or hands on the keyboard, the ones going out and delivering every day to customers both internally and externally. But leaders need to take on the hard work of changing how they make decisions, how they behave with each other, and how they work together to get through the challenges of moving forward, growing successfully, and delivering on ambitious strategies. When leaders lean in, transformation becomes reality.

> **Leaders love to change other people, but they don't love changing themselves.**

The whole purpose of taking the time to define *HOW* to lead and work together is to drive activation to new ways of working that drive different outcomes, and that isn't about process, technology, or structures. It is about how, as humans, each member of the team is committing to doing things differently together. As a leader, consider looking inward and answering the following questions:

» If you don't need to change how you lead, are you really transforming your organization?

» How could you take ownership of changing how you lead before asking your people to work differently?

» How can you support your peers and other team leaders on this quest for alignment to ambitious goals?

» How can you visibly demonstrate to your colleagues that you are changing your influencers to drive different results?

Your turn: Can you think of questions you should be asking yourself and your colleagues about how you are working and leading together to create and support progress in your organization? Have a conversation with your colleagues about the questions you need to ask each other.

Remember that there are no fully correct or final answers to these questions or to the list of questions. Because we are all human and live in a dynamically changing world, alignment is a constant flow that requires attention and care. As new people join a team, as things happen that shift power dynamics and relationships, as the business changes, alignment to how to work together can change over time. Knowing the questions you want to consider will help you pay attention to the behaviors and decisions that will get you to the outcomes you want.

The shifts we talked about in the last chapter are the sometimes small but powerful ways of working that build the foundation for individual and team commitments that fuel decision-making and behaviors that drive outcomes. By committing to *HOW* to lead together through the lens of influencers, you can support yourself and others in getting where you need to be to deliver new outcomes. In business, this equals transformative success for leaders, team members, and businesses.

Team Commitments

For teams, the question of *HOW* to lead and work together to deliver on your WHAT and WHY is answered and made visible to others through new ways of working that everyone commits to using. *Ways of working*, which we express as *team commitments*, are an articulation of the decisions and behaviors that will create new outcomes for the team as a whole. When you know your *team commitments*, and you know the ways in

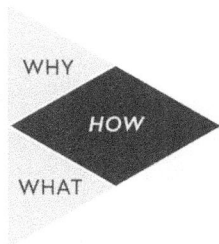

which the *influencers* need to shift to support your collective actions, you can consistently commit to new decisions and behaviors that drive different outcomes—even in high-pressure situations.

This is the essence of the *HOW* of the Diamond Triangle—*clarity* and *connection* on your individual and joint influencers that need to shift, *commitment* to new ways of working that drive decision-making and behaviors, and the *courage* to do things differently.

The action piece of the Behavior Model is where new ways of working are identified and codified into team commitments that translate into new decisions and behaviors, leading to new results.

On teams, decisions and behaviors are guided by our ways of working together. Ways of working create enough clarity for people to know how to shift their behavior, but they aren't prescriptive and directive to precise situations because people maintain agency and apply critical thinking to respond appropriately for the context of the moment. Different teams need different kinds of ways of working, and they will fall somewhere between abstract and specific.

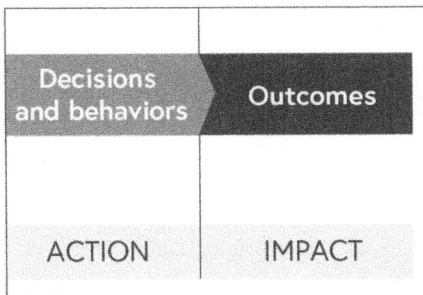

Image 4.5: Focus on Decisions, Behaviors, and Outcomes

The diagram below shows the sweet spot for ways of working that become effective team commitments.

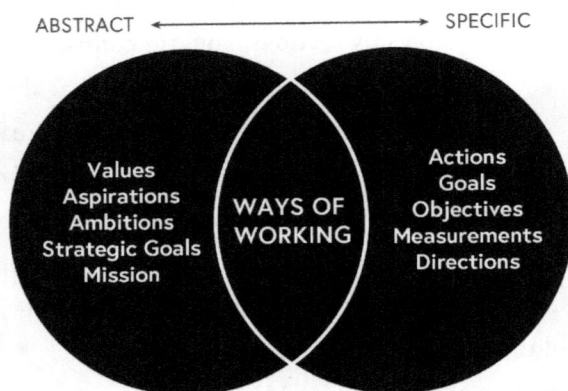

ABSTRACT ←————————————→ SPECIFIC

Values
Aspirations
Ambitions
Strategic Goals
Mission

WAYS OF
WORKING

Actions
Goals
Objectives
Measurements
Directions

Image 5.1: Ways of Working Venn Diagram

Notice that team commitments are not abstract, generalized value statements or vague promises of idealized behaviors. They are informed by your influencers and specific to how your team works together to deliver outcomes. They may include specific actions, goals, objectives, measurements, and directions, but they don't have to. They should be defined at a level where the team can constructively talk about them and see/feel/hear if they are being upheld or not. In general, good team commitments are reminders to *do things*, not to *be things*, and as a team, you can discuss and evaluate how you are doing and if you are driving new outcomes as a result.

I always encourage leaders to remember that team commitments are meant to be in service to their specific needs as a team. They don't need to be universally applicable; they aren't meant to replace values or leadership competencies across the company, and they won't work if they are diluted to make them good corporate-speak. In ideating and finalizing team commitments, they often get refined. But they shouldn't become so generalized that they lose all meaning to the people who are crafting them.

It is in the process of developing team commitments together that team members build a shared understanding and shared language of what team commitments mean. Shortcutting that process or outsourcing it to others will only result in failure. A good facilitator can help smooth the process, but at Karrikins Group, when we partner with clients to build team commitments, we always remind them that the work is *with them for them, not by us to them*—the work is done in the room with the team.

> In ideating and finalizing team commitments, they often get refined. But they shouldn't become so generalized that they lose all meaning to the people who are crafting them.

The Measurement Trap

As you start to develop team commitments, there are a few things to keep in mind: Sometimes clients want an obsessive level of measurement for their team commitments. But that is rarely necessary, and it can be counterproductive. High achievers have a habit of wanting to work with a scorecard that tracks organizational factors instead of working on individual mindsets and group dynamics that need to shift. That's a difficult habit to break. It is easy to think *What gets measured gets done*, but it is also the case that *what gets measured gets manipulated.* When your goal is to get the green dot on the scorecard, you risk making poor decisions just to get the dopamine hit.

> When your goal is to get the green dot on the scorecard, you risk making poor decisions just to get the dopamine hit.

That's why team commitments should be observable but not necessarily countable. Team members know, qualitatively, if they are honoring their commitments. If the right vocabulary has been developed early in this process by bringing clarity and connection to the influencers, a team will have the language to discuss how well they are delivering on the decisions and behaviors they've committed to.

In general, I like to assess how team members feel they are doing when it comes to delivering on team commitments rather than measuring how many times they take a specific action. I'd rather see teams identify ways of working together that are specific enough to be visible when they are happening and when they aren't, without getting so detailed that they end up getting crushed under the weight of a massive scorecard meant to keep track of them like Big Brother. Scorecards have a time and place, but not here.

Impressive Versus Effective

I generally discourage clients from having big, impressive team commitments with idealized words like *trust*, *integrity*, and *respect*. Those are too ambiguous to inspire new decisions and behaviors. The most successful team commitments are in that sweet spot between ambiguous and specific, with a focus on the necessary mindsets, group dynamics, and trade-offs that need to shift rather than the organizational factors or blockers that need to change.

Check out this handful of team commitments different clients have created with us. Keep in mind that because they were fully engaged in doing the work together, these have deep meaning for them, even if they seem simple to you as an outsider:

» Simplify relentlessly

» Discuss, debate, decide, move ahead

» Listen more, talk less

» Consistently ask who else could help

» Put in the time together to connect as a team

» Bring levity daily

» Show up with grit and grace

Situationally Appropriate

Team commitments don't need to be big, enduring statements about idealized behaviors that never go out of style. They may be situational, like when SnackInvasion needed to transform their technology platforms. They may be a muscle that needs focus and attention, like when Sara's TT1 needed to be better at collaboration. Either way, once the muscle is built, it can move into maintenance mode, and the team can repeat the process to align on different team commitments as a way to level up their leadership and advance new priorities. And there certainly may be long-lasting team commitments to new ways of working that become deeply embedded in the culture and leadership and guide the organization over time. This is where the focus can be changed up, depending on the situation, the need, and the people involved.

There is no one answer to what a "good" team commitment is, because it depends on the situation and the team. But there are ways to think about stronger or weaker team commitments that will help drive changes to behavior and decision-making, inspiring action that changes the outcomes you are trying to deliver.

The *P-HOWS* Model of Team Commitments

I think of strong team commitments as being *P-HOWS*. These are *powerful HOWs* that include five characteristics:

1. Powerful impact

2. Human centric

3. Observable (but not always measurable)

4. Within the team

5. Sticky (easy to remember)

Here is a simple chart defining each of the above five elements:

POWERFUL IMPACT
Powerful impact means that the commitment will drive meaningful new outcomes for the team and the business.

HUMAN CENTRIC
Human centric means focusing on influencing behaviors and decisions, not on systems and processes.

OBSERVABLE
Observable means you know when you are doing it and can have a conversation about how it is impacting your desired outcomes.

WITHIN THE TEAM
Within the team means that the group of people creating the commitment are the ones who need to implement it. It isn't for someone else to do.

STICKY
Sticky simply means that the commitment is easy to remember and bring into conversation with others.

Let's look at examples of each—I've included the "color" versions of several from clients we've worked with, but they are often abbreviated in conversation to the headline. Keep in mind that a good team commitment has all five characteristics, but to help illustrate the concepts I've lined them up with characteristics they highlight.

POWERFUL IMPACT

Weak team commitment:
We will become a fully aligned team working with one voice all the time.

Strong team commitment: One level deeper
We pause to go one level deeper on trade-offs.

HUMAN CENTRIC

Weak team commitment:
We trust and respect one another.

Strong team commitment: Grit and grace
We have the grit to push back respectfully and the grace to accept decisions and follow through on what's necessary.

OBSERVABLE

Weak team commitment:
We will build a process to debate issues and measure the number of decisions we debate.

Strong team commitment: Discuss, debate, decide
We have the conversation, ask questions in the room, and support one another outside of the room.

WITHIN THE TEAM

Weak team commitment:
We will invest in our people by creating collaboration incentives to ensure they become a strong next generation of leaders.

Strong team commitment: Connect the dots
We connect the dots by discussing the broader impacts of key decisions before moving forward.

STICKY

Weak team commitment:
When dealing with complex issues, we will follow a prescribed sixteen-step process for discussion and debate before completing a multistep voting process to arrive at a conclusion together.

Strong team commitment: Simplify relentlessly
Take the time together to deselect, prioritize, and say no to unnecessary complexity.

Now it's your turn. Think about ways you and your colleagues could work together to shift some of your influencers to drive new behaviors and decisions. How could you establish a few new ways of working that would meaningfully change your team's decisions and behaviors to drive new outcomes? These should be team commitments with the characteristics of *P-HOWS* that you can talk through and craft based on the *influencers* you've identified together. Consider examples pertaining to *your* team; don't worry about needing to come up with something that is universal for your organization. Don't hesitate to grab a piece of paper or note your ideas here.

P-HOW WORKSHEET

Possible Team Commitments	Powerful Impact Able to drive meaningful new outcomes for the team and the business.	Human Centric Focuses on influencing behaviors and decisions, not on systems and processes.	Observable You know when you are doing it and how it is impacting your desired outcomes.	Within the Team The group of people creating the commitment are the ones who need to implement it.	Sticky It is easy to remember and bring into conversation with others.
	☐	☐	☐	☐	☐
	☐	☐	☐	☐	☐
	☐	☐	☐	☐	☐
	☐	☐	☐	☐	☐
	☐	☐	☐	☐	☐

Image 5.2: *P-HOW* Worksheet

Remember that it's easy to move from the idea of you and your leaders transforming how you lead to how other people need to work differently or to idealized behaviors that are aspirational but impractical. And once you do that, you've lost momentum to do the hard and courageous work of figuring out how to change yourselves. It also generally turns into a marketing exercise, where people try to cram in lofty words like *innovative* or *trust* without any real substance behind how to bring those big words to life. Crafting team commitments isn't a theoretical exercise about perfect behavior; it's a practical exercise that answers the

> **Focus your *P-HOWS* on mindsets and group dynamics more than organizational factors to keep the emphasis on behavior change for leaders.**

question of *HOW* this specific team can lead differently to create new outcomes in a given situation. My mantra for team commitments is to lean into "simple/better," while being robust enough that they make sense to the whole team.

Keep in mind, team commitments start as being specifically for the people who created them. They don't have to be broadly applicable to everyone in the organization. Often they are helpful for anyone, but their purpose is to help leaders on a specific team know how to lead together to create targeted new outcomes. Focus on the commitments that are best in service to the team, and then, if it makes sense to roll them out more broadly, you can work on cascading them in the organization.

By asking *HOW* we need to lead or work together differently, you get to the heart of how the team connects the dots and takes advantage of the spaces between them in the business. Imagine if Sony Music, Nokia Mobile, Blockbuster, or Kodak had ways of working that had allowed them to connect across their businesses easily and consistently. The world might be a very different place today.

Team Commitments in Practice

Let's take a look at how Sara's TT1 and Sandy and Jordon's leadership team at SnackInvasion built out their team commitments based on the influencers they identified.

CASE STUDY ────────────────────────────────

Tech Team 1

Remember that Sara's TT1 had been struggling to collaborate effectively as a team of leaders. Sara was having conversations with them about how they defined collaboration, and they identified the mindsets, group dynamics, trade-offs, and blockers that helped them define collaboration more precisely. Organizational factors like time zones were identified but not solved in this process—there is no solution for time zones, but making the challenge visible was helpful in navigating the difficulties of multiple time zones.

As Sara and her team talked through these influencers over a series of discussions, they discovered they had a lot in common in terms of how they oriented toward the idea of collaboration. Some of their stories included:

» A shared sense that it is a nice-to-have but that practically, it doesn't contribute to better outcomes and probably isn't worth the time commitment from one another

» A shared belief that they would have to give up decision authority if they asked another leader to collaborate with them on a solution

» An all-or-nothing type of belief that either they created a process for collaboration that they executed perfectly every time, or they didn't bother with it at all

» A collective story that in the past they had created processes for collaboration that hadn't worked, which was frustrating and demoralizing, because they didn't like to fail or waste their time

MINDSETS	GROUP DYNAMICS	ORGANIZATIONAL FACTORS
If I ask someone else to participate, I give up my right to make the decision myself.	We stay in our lanes, respecting the boundaries of our roles and expecting others to do the same.	Time zones make it hard to connect quickly and effectively.
Our areas of the business are very different, so I don't have anything to add to another's discussions.	Everyone is already booked in back-to-back meetings, so having another one just to say we collaborated doesn't make sense.	Execs often pit us against one another by asking multiple people to solve the same problem.
I want to fully control the narrative when I'm presenting, so questions aren't welcome. I want to get in and out of the spotlight fast.	We don't have the right to ask people in other areas questions when we aren't experts or informed.	Our organizational structure makes it tough to share.

Team members also had a few exceptional examples of positive experiences with collaboration and how they experienced the support and the opportunity to connect with their colleagues. They pointed to examples of discovering someone else on the team had already solved a problem or that they were both working on the same issue at the same time, so they were able to consolidate and be more effective together.

From these stories and examples, they identified some specific mindsets, group dynamics, and organizational factors that were getting in the way of aligning on collaboration across the team. We talked about some of these in the last chapter, but let's take a deeper dive here.

These key influencers fuel the secondary influencers of trade-offs and blockers. TT1 identified some of their trade-offs and blockers to collaboration as:

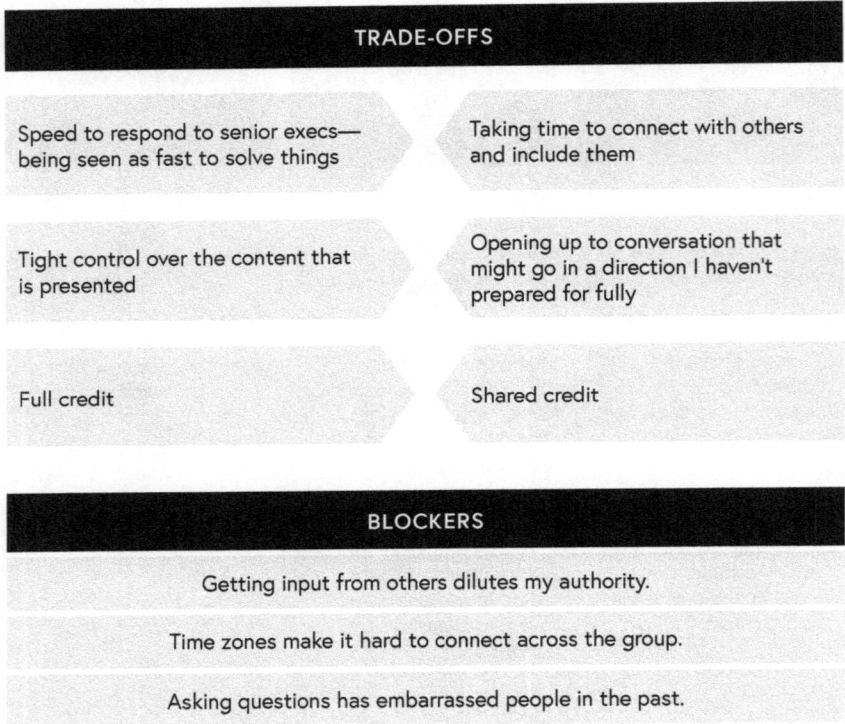

TRADE-OFFS	
Speed to respond to senior execs—being seen as fast to solve things	Taking time to connect with others and include them
Tight control over the content that is presented	Opening up to conversation that might go in a direction I haven't prepared for fully
Full credit	Shared credit

BLOCKERS
Getting input from others dilutes my authority.
Time zones make it hard to connect across the group.
Asking questions has embarrassed people in the past.

As they got deeper into these key and secondary influencers over a series of conversations, TT1 was able to create more shared understanding about the impact their default mindsets and group dynamics were having on how the team made decisions and behaved in certain situations, like when an executive team called with an urgent request, they needed to solve a technology issue, or as they prepared for QBRs. As they built this shared understanding together over time, the members of TT1 were able to identify a handful of small and powerful shifts they could make to create new actions when faced with situations where collaboration would be impactful to the outcomes they wanted to create. Their three main team commitments ended up being:

1. **Check in first**. When a call comes from a senior executive who needs something, connect with the team to see if anyone else has insight or is working on the problem.

2. **Respect the invitation**. Understand that contribution is welcome but doesn't change who owns the decision.

3. **Be expansive, not embarrassing**. Pay attention to the difference between asking a question that expands the group's thinking and embarrassing the person being asked the question.

For TT1, these new team commitments provided a powerful touchstone to start to shift into new ways of working together that would support a more collaborative team experience. They may seem like words on a page to you, but to the team, they had deep meaning and context because of the time they'd spent in conversation, talking through them and developing them together.

CASE STUDY

SnackInvasion

Recall that SnackInvasion was embarking on a high-pressure, high-stakes transformation that required consolidating major systems across the company. The executive leadership team needed to be on the same page as they moved forward, and they needed to challenge how they were leading together during this difficult effort.

The CEO, Jordon, and the CFO, Sandy, got the executive team together to talk through what was ahead of them. They were able to tap into several stories across the executive team that were getting in the way:

» We just aren't good at this kind of transformation. We keep trying, failing, and this won't be any different.

» If I support this effort, I'll lose important functionality in my own area or region.

» I've already invested in a system that works well for me. Why should I have to carve out a budget for the areas that haven't done the work?

» I can't afford to dedicate people to this effort; everyone is too busy already, and I know it will just be wasted time.

Because the leadership team knew the transformation was important, they were reluctant to give voice to these deep concerns about the impact on their areas. Yet these stories were fueling their mindsets and group dynamics and were reflected in their organizational factors.

As the team slowly started to move beyond simply agreeing that transformation was a good idea, they started exploring what it would mean to align and deliver together. Through further conversation, the team got deeper into what they had identified.

MINDSETS	GROUP DYNAMICS	ORGANIZATIONAL FACTORS
I need to protect my people from extra work so I don't get them involved in this kind of thing.	It is better to find a way (even if it is creative) to be in "green" status than to honestly share what's going on.	The budgeting process makes supporting transformation tough.
I contribute by making sure my area delivers what it needs to, no matter what.	We keep our program status meetings fast and efficient rather than having productive dialogue.	Transformation support is allocated unevenly across our regions.

As with TT1, these key influencers fueled the secondary influencers of trade-offs and blockers. SnackInvasion identified some of their trade-offs and blockers to transformation as:

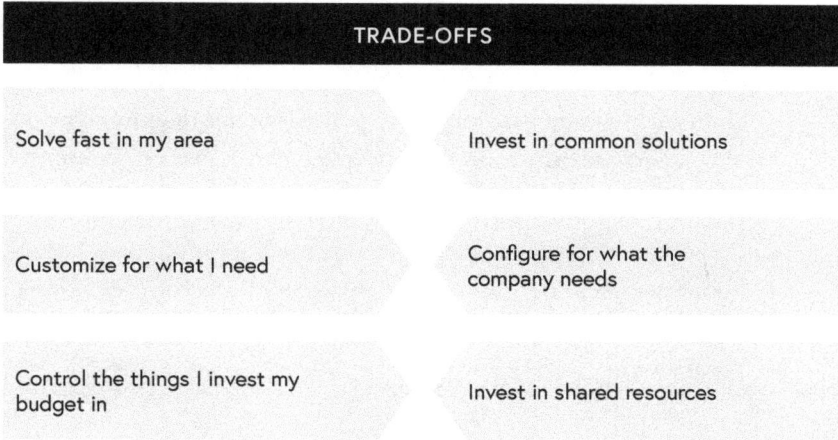

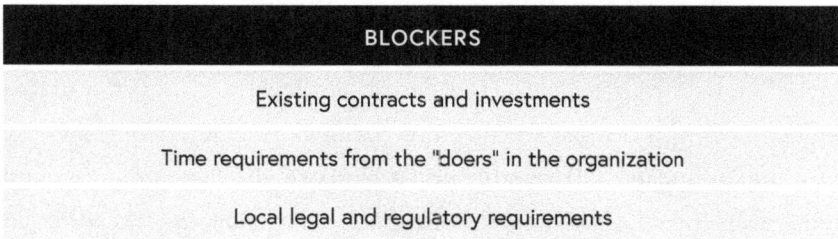

TRADE-OFFS	
Solve fast in my area	Invest in common solutions
Customize for what I need	Configure for what the company needs
Control the things I invest my budget in	Invest in shared resources

BLOCKERS
Existing contracts and investments
Time requirements from the "doers" in the organization
Local legal and regulatory requirements

As they talked through these key and secondary influencers over a series of conversations, the SnackInvasion team built out shifts that would have a meaningful impact on how they led together while also being within reach of actually doing. From those shifts, they came up with the following four team commitments to help them activate their leadership of the transformation to drive different outcomes than what had been achieved historically:

1. **We aren't so different**. Visibility and transparency across our regions will help us all to be better leaders and fuel our growth as a company.

2. **We are all heading to the same destination**. We are each going to struggle differently, but we have to engage in the struggle and support one another.

3. **Challenge ourselves first, then our people**. We must lead from a conviction that joining together is better than working alone. And we can't expect our people to work in ways we aren't working in as leaders.

4. **Have the conversation**. If we don't talk with one another about what's going on, we can't create solutions together. Don't implement solutions for your region unilaterally; bring them to the team.

For SnackInvasion, these new team commitments were a catalyst to changing how the leadership team worked together to transform their organization. As with the team commitments from TT1, they may seem like words on a page to you, but to the leaders, they had a shared understanding as a result of the conversations they'd had along the way to developing them. They represented shifts to the key and secondary influencers that had kept the team stuck in agreement—the dreaded Failure Gap.

Small Steps Drive Big Results

There is power in small, consistent actions over time. Don't imagine that one big conversation about committing to new ways of working is going to suddenly fix things. Catalytic changes rarely stick, and team commitments aren't magical. You must breathe life into change slowly and consistently. This takes small, consistent actions over time, including the action of having authentic, challenging conversations as a team through the lens of your influencers. Sara and her TT1 team started using team commitments in their standing meetings. When a team member described a problem they had recently solved, Sara asked, "Did you check in first?" In team meetings, they became more comfortable asking for input, often prefacing requests with laughter and saying, "Respect the invitation!" They gently reminded one another to "expand, not embarrass" one another when they had probing questions. As often happens with this work, it became fun for them to find ways to bring the team commitments forward and use them to help lubricate the connections between team members.

While positive change can be energizing, it isn't always easy. There are situations where team commitments become weaponized, and people become snarky. Imagine a SnackInvasion team member who is determined to stay on their old system saying "You didn't have the conversation" when asked to support something in a meeting. Or a team member saying "Respect the invitation" in a sneering way when someone pushes for a new idea in a collaboration session. It is unfortunate when this happens. We typically expect better from our leaders. But we are all human, and sometimes we aren't at our best.

When weaponization occurs, all the value of the work done to align on *HOW* to lead together evaporates. As the old expression goes, trust is built in drops and lost in buckets, and the connection that is established during the intentional dialogue process of creating the team commitments dissipates quickly. In those moments, the rest of the team needs to lean in and "notice and name" the situation to deal with it directly. Otherwise, it festers and gets worse over time. If you've done the work and invested the time in building your *HOW*, the team will course correct quickly rather than getting sucked into historically bad behaviors like weaponizing team commitments. It takes courage to speak up and address poor behavior without disparaging the leader involved. Show patience, give people grace, and also hold them to a high standard when it comes to team commitments.

When creating your team commitments, keep things straightforward. Trying to make them too impressive, lofty, or universally appealing is an ambiguity trap. Avoid value statements that read like a top-ten list of job requirements for saints—things like *respect, trust, integrity, consideration, kindness, generosity,* and *joy.* These are all great words, but without a shared understanding of what they mean in the context of a team, they don't change behavior. Be specific and consistent, taking one small step at a time.

I often talk with teams who want to do this work fast. They feel like they can "knock it out" quickly in a single working session and be done with it. But that's not how humans work. Shortcutting the process and just trying to "get it done" means you aren't spending enough time in conversation with one another to create shared meaning and commitment to the new ways of working. Both TT1 and SnackInvasion spent several hours together in sessions, working over three to four months, discussing and debating their team commitments to support new outcomes. In that intentional dialogue, they did the work to make the invisible visible and to develop a new language for working together. The conversations they had included:

» Identifying the stories they were holding on to

» Exploring and clarifying the influencers of mindsets, group dynamics, organizational factors, trade-offs, and blockers

» Articulating shifts in the influencers that would drive new decisions and behaviors for the team

» Codifying those shifts in team commitments that were visible (although not necessarily measurable)

If you want to build alignment to new ways of working together, you will need to have these conversations as well. I can't say it enough: This work doesn't get done in a catalytic session. It requires a series of discussions over time to create shared meaning across the team and establish commitment to making the shifts that pull you out of the Failure Gap and into alignment. Then it takes courage to consistently do small things differently over time, and that is what ultimately changes the trajectory of success.

Remember that you have access to additional resources to support your conversations on our resources page. These resources can help you and your team to have the tough discussions about what's holding you back from aligning and taking action on your highest priorities, biggest goals, and most ambitious missions.

KEY TAKEAWAYS

» During times of transformation, you can't leave change up to the doers in the organization. Leaders must start by changing how they lead together if they want to transform the company.

» You will get further faster through small, powerful shifts than with giant pivots that people struggle to deliver.

» Action is in the behaviors and decisions we make. These are fueled by the influencers in the Behavior Model, and they drive the outcomes we create.

» Ways of working help establish new decisions and behaviors for leaders to adopt. These ways of working should be somewhere between abstract and specific, depending on the situation at hand.

» Ways of working become team commitments when the team has refined them into touchstone language that they can hold one another accountable to delivering.

» You should be aware of a few traps when developing team commitments:

- Measurability: Not all things need to be counted. Team commitments should be observable but not necessarily measurable.

- Impressive but ineffective language: Idealized behavior statements don't tend to change behaviors. Team commitments should be in practical language.

- Generalities: This work should be specific for the team and situation, not so general that it loses applicability to what needs to be accomplished.

» *P-HOWS* are the characteristics of well-written team commitments that represent powerful *HOW* statements. *P-HOWS* stands for:

- Powerful impact

- Human centric

- Observable (but not always measurable)

- Within the team

- Sticky (easy to remember)

» Beware of team commitments becoming weaponized. If this starts to happen, the team needs to make it visible and deal with it quickly.

» You must commit time and effort to doing this work together as a team over time. It cannot be accomplished in a single catalytic experience or conversation.

Check out www.makehowmatter.com/worksheets
for more resources.

Optimism is not believing things will be easy; it is believing in your ability to do hard things.

6

Implementation: Bringing Your *HOW* to Life

Courage doesn't always roar. Sometimes courage is the quiet voice at the end of the day saying, "I will try again tomorrow."
—**Mary Anne Radmacher, writer, educator, artist**

OVER THE LAST FEW SECTIONS, we have looked at bringing clarity and connection to the influencers of decisions and behaviors, and the power of defining shifts in mindsets, group dynamics, and trade-offs to change how you lead together while also identifying organizational factors and blockers that get in the way of new ways of working. We've talked about new, shared ways of working, or team commitments, based on the shifts in the influencers you identify. We've looked at *HOW*, through the intentional dialogue required to define your shifts and ways of working, you and your colleagues can build a shared language for tackling your biggest hurdles to leading together, making it easier to work as a team. All of this is in service to completing your Diamond Triangle by getting as clear on *HOW* to lead together as you are on your WHAT and your WHY. You are well on your way!

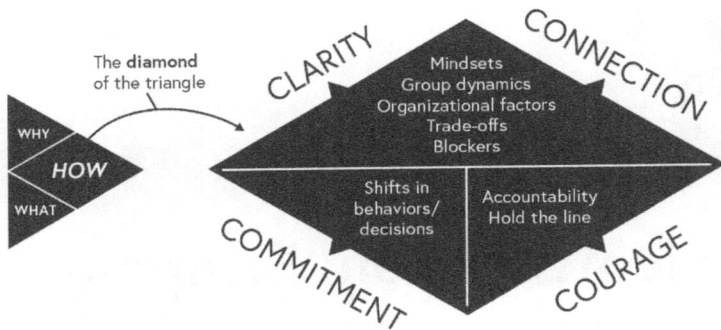

Image 2.8: The Diamond of the Triangle

But the gravitational pull of business as usual is incredibly strong. Just like the personal habits that keep people eating ice cream and pizza when they say they want to be healthier or that kept me scrolling on Instagram when I was meant to be learning Spanish, the habituated patterns of teams are easy to revert to when things get tough. That's why people decide to stick with old processes to ensure reliability instead of trying something innovative, or hold off on a new go-to-market strategy and instead use the same old approaches to deliver just enough to squeak by on quarterly numbers, or decide to go it alone instead of engaging a colleague to help with something.

Understanding your WHY, WHAT, and *HOW* are vital to change. Knowing the importance of behaviors, decisions, and new ways of working will take you and your team leaps and bounds toward success. But having the courage to stay true to *HOW* to lead together is what moves you through the Failure Gap, so let's dive into the nitty-gritty of when it gets hard (because it always does). Let's have a look at a few ways you can fuel the courage to hold the line as a team.

Collective Accountability

Holding yourself and others accountable to actions that might be hard to execute is incredibly difficult for a lot of people. I've worked with traditionally heroic people who are indisputably courageous in the face of imminent danger—veterans, police officers, and public speakers, to name a few! I have watched these incredible people falter when they have to talk to a colleague about an inconsistent behavior or speak up about a misaligned decision. Holding other people accountable in a positive and actionable way can feel like a steep hill to climb, and even the bravest among us struggle with it.

The good news is, if your team has done the work through intentional dialogue to build a shared language for how to talk about desired shifts and the impact of misaligned decisions and behaviors, you will collectively find the courage to leap the Failure Gap and deliver new outcomes. Having shifts identified and team commitments codified gives people the language to create accountability for themselves and others. Creating patterns and routines in your group dynamics to support transparency and accountability is also a powerful way to ensure you don't lose sight of aligned action.

I encourage teams to establish a cadence—perhaps quarterly—for checking in on accountability to *HOW* they are leading together. An easy way to do that is to have standard questions you ask one another every quarter about your team commitments. You can also use these questions when specific situations come up where it is hard to stay aligned.

Have a conversation with your team about what questions you should get comfortable asking each other to drive accountability to your team commitments. Here are five questions to get you started:

1. Which of our team commitments have the biggest impact on our decisions as a team?

2. What's one example of something we did differently because we are aligned on *HOW* to lead together?

3. What mindsets, group dynamics, and trade-offs are still holding us back?

4. Which organizational factors or blockers need our time and attention?

5. What needs to be adjusted or modified based on where we are now?

Because team commitments are specific to your team and situation, accountability questions can be tuned for your environment. Consider adding another few questions you and your leadership team should discuss. Talk with your team about the questions they think you need to discuss together to promote accountability to your team commitments.

At Karrikins Group, we work with our clients to conduct routine accountability assessments that help leaders to see and hear about potential issues in a more objective way. By creating routines around accountability, including the timing and questions you ask, you build an alignment orientation. It's a fluid way of leading where you check in, adjust, and set the standard on a regular basis. It reduces the need to spend social capital on drawing attention to where the team is coming up short and makes the conversation more accessible and acceptable to people who might have missed their goals or who aren't showing up as well as they should. It establishes a group norm for accountability and having difficult conversations with one another about how the team and individuals are bringing the team commitments to life.

And sometimes, leaders just need to take a deep breath and have the conversation with their colleagues about accountability, reconnecting everyone with the work that has been done and why it is so important to create the outcomes everyone should be working toward. I can't solve for that being difficult, but doing this work together does make it a little bit easier by bringing clarity and connection to what behaviors are expected.

Role Clarity in Decision-Making

The courage to lead differently can be held back when people have uncertainty in their roles, particularly around decision-making. This usually comes up when working through individual mindsets and group dynamics around who gets to make decisions, how often decisions are overridden or renegotiated, and who has the loudest or softest voice in the room. It can also appear when teams say they need to make faster decisions together.

I have worked with dozens of team leaders who say they want more velocity in decision-making, but they don't know how to have the conversations they need to support getting to a decision. This often results in the Failure Gap—agreement that something should be done, but taking no action because the decision-making process didn't work well.

Many years ago, as a young consultant, I learned about the value of role clarity in decision-making. In basic terms, *role clarity* is knowing who is responsible for what. At the time, RACI charts were all the rage. RACI charts were meant to help teams identify who was *responsible*, *accountable*, *consulted*, and *informed* about a decision. Other variations with different root words have emerged over time, but the outcome has been the same— someone puts a lot of time and energy into creating charts that are rarely used. That's because there isn't enough intentional dialogue around what the different terms mean and how it feels to be in one of the columns. It's also because humans are complicated, decisions aren't straightforward, and there are too many variables to capture in a static chart.

I prefer a common alliteration that is used in decision-making to clarify who has a *voice*, a *vote*, and a *veto*. The role of the voice is to speak out and offer perspective. The role of the vote is to have a say in the chosen action. And the role the veto plays is to make the final decision to move forward. I first heard of this approach many years ago. (It has been around a long time, and I can't source it properly.) Whenever I've used it with clients, it has quickly changed how they talk about making decisions. It has been my experience that this mnemonic is easy to remember and apply, making it far more useful than a RACI chart, where it seems like someone is always asking "Wait, which one am I for this decision?"

So, how does this work? It's simple. When your team is making a difficult decision, clarify the voice, vote, and veto roles to smooth out the discussion and create the space for tough conversations.

When someone knows which of these roles they have, it increases their confidence in contributing, because they understand where they fit into the decision-making process. It reduces frustration from people who might think they have a vote but only have a voice in the process. It also alleviates anxiety from people who want to make sure they don't lose their decision rights by establishing up front that they maintain a veto or final say in what happens.

> When your team is making a difficult decision, clarify the voice, vote, and veto roles to smooth out the discussion and create the space for tough conversations.

Whatever approach you use, creating transparency and a shared understanding of decision-making processes is tremendously helpful in knowing *HOW* to lead together. When people can place themselves in the discussion, they can contribute more confidently. The outcome is that the team has more robust discussions about how decisions are aligned or misaligned, and they make more informed choices about how to move forward through that lens.

Pushing for Specifics

Sometimes, as we get toward the end of building a Diamond Triangle with a client, we see leaders get a little nervous about the new decisions and behaviors that will be expected of them, including finding the courage to be a part of something instead of going alone. Leaders can have trouble finding their footing with new ways of working because they struggle with:

» The comfort of the status quo

» A fear of losing autonomy and decision rights

» The temptation of staying focused only on their own areas

» Continuing to deliver on old metrics when new ones are required

» Having the courage to speak up in a meeting instead of outside of it

» Feeling too busy to continue to engage in dialogue with colleagues

Push colleagues (and yourself) to be specific about how you are going to lead something together so that you make the new decisions and behaviors visible. That includes normalizing the discussion of these kinds of resistance points. By being able to talk about them as a team, you can support one another in working through them.

Hopefully, as you've worked together to build the *HOW* of your Diamond Triangle, you've gotten better at being in dialogue with one another, and you can talk about these struggles in honest, open ways. If you feel like you or your colleagues aren't quite there yet, keep at it—these things take time. But remember something I mentioned earlier—ambiguity protects the status quo. Don't let leaders hide behind vague promises or loose agreements without acknowledging the hard work they need to do as leaders.

Beware of the Power of *Fine*

At Karrikins Group, we have a team commitment around *being in pursuit of better*. This commitment is language we use in decision-making all the time. If we are debating whether to upgrade a solution we have, we might lean toward the *status quo*, especially if we are busy with delivery work for clients. If someone feels like we are misaligned to our team commitment, all they have to do is ask the question: Are we staying in pursuit of better? This shift changes the conversation in positive ways and ensures we don't cut off debate too soon. Ultimately, I make the decision about whether we do the upgrade (I have the veto), and the answer isn't always yes. But by grounding in our team commitment to be in pursuit of better, the entire team can be transparent about how we prioritize our time, money, and resources. And everyone has a voice or a vote in the discussion.

We have to talk about it very intentionally, because it is easy to feel like things are fine, but being fine is often a bigger risk than being in terrible shape—when things are bad, there's a big incentive to change. When things are *fine*, it's tough to risk dependability and success to try something new. The pull of the status quo is such a challenge—the incredible power of inertia will always drag everyone back into old ways of working together that feel comfortable and deliver the same predictable results.

Over time, the system—a team and the organization—will work phenomenally hard to maintain stasis and avoid risk as long as things are OK—the fear of going from *fine* to *bad* overrides the energy of going from *fine* to *amazing*. The trouble with settling for things being fine is that one day you wake up and they aren't fine, and it's a shock to the whole system. Being fine blinds you to opportunities and risks in the market because you are so focused on reliability that you miss them until it is too late.

Think back to the Karrikins Alignment Maturity Model I shared at the beginning of this book. You may remember that I said level 3 is often the riskiest. It is where things feel OK because individuals are delivering and things feel pretty good, but the connective fiber isn't there to take advantage of investments and opportunities or manage risks. If one of your team's challenges relates to being comfortable with being fine, revisit the Behavior Model and get clear about what *better outcomes* would look like. Start by asking yourself the following questions:

» What are the mindsets and group dynamics keeping us settled—*fine*—instead of going after more ambitious outcomes?

» What beliefs and fears do we have about the future, trying new things, and the risk of failure?

» What trade-offs need to be made visible and negotiated differently?

» What organizational factors and blockers are in the way, and how could we navigate them differently?

» How are we making decisions and behaving as leaders—what are our deeply habituated patterns that need to be challenged?

As you work through these questions, identify the small shifts that might help shake things up a bit for the team. Are there different questions you could ask in team meetings? Are there benchmarks you could explore in other industries? Are there lessons you could learn from other areas of the company? Often letting go of *fine* starts with being more curious about how other people are doing things, so building leadership habits around curiosity may be a place to start.

Taking It Further

We often have clients who are so happy with their leaders' team commitments, they want to cascade them to their vertical teams. While delegating the creation of your team commitments doesn't work, *cascading* is appropriate under specific circumstances. This is something we encourage, as long as it is done through intentional dialogue and not through email or slideware. If you want to share your commitments with people who didn't help build them, it is incumbent on you to stick with the mantra "talk, don't tell." By that I mean you, as a leader, must engage your vertical teams in conversations where you share the story behind how the team commitments were created. The powerful understanding you have is only shared through sensemaking that happens through dialogue.

This includes sharing:

» The types of conversations you and your colleagues had

» The debates you and your leadership team engaged in

» The mindsets, group dynamics, trade-offs, and blockers you identified

» Why you prioritized the actions you listed in your team commitments

» What you are struggling with personally in the shifts to your own leadership

You need to provide situations and examples that help people understand and connect with the content as more than words on a page. Helping to onboard new people to team commitments is *not* a one-and-done exercise conducted via PowerPoint. It requires you, as a leader, to have fluency in your team commitments so you use them in regular conversations. We often suggest that leaders partner up with other people on their horizontal/peer team to cascade their commitments vertically. Doing so creates solidarity, alignment, and visible connection at the leadership level from the beginning.

Know That Sometimes Misalignment Is OK

Your Diamond Triangle, with its WHAT, WHY, and *HOW*, doesn't tell you the right answer for navigating tough decisions, but it does guide the discussions you have, so that even if you arrive at a misaligned decision, everyone knows the trade-offs and why you opted to go in a different direction.

It is actually OK if you make a misaligned decision that doesn't support your stated desired outcomes, as long as you have the right conversations and do it in an informed and transparent way. It is inauthentic to manipulate the logic of a decision to make it appear aligned when, in fact, it isn't. Don't waste valuable time, energy, and thinking on figuring out how to do that—instead, have the courage to talk through the reasons why the decision is misaligned and whether the team is willing to accept the realities and consequences of that.

For example, if a team is struggling with product innovation, they may be trading innovation for reliability because there is a strong organizational preference for reliable results. Let's imagine they align on an outcome where they invest in more innovative product development, and they build team commitments to support that outcome. That doesn't mean they say yes to every idea that comes along! If someone comes up with an innovative new product that jeopardizes the team's ability to appropriately support existing clients, the decision may be to pass on the idea. That's OK, as long as the conversation that fuels the decision is made through the lens of the influencers and team commitments. Team members can use the language of the team commitment to innovation to spark the conversation and check in on the influencers that may be driving the decision, but they aren't required to always choose to invest in innovation. The point is to shift the conversations so you are challenging any deeply habituated choices in productive ways.

In that example, by being transparent and authentic about the trade-off, leaders establish new decision-making guardrails. They use their voices in a positive, productive manner. They make visible the standard they are holding for operational reliability and what levels of innovation are tolerable. And they start to experience the degree to which they may be uncomfortably stuck in their ways, because they have to say out loud that they are choosing current customers over innovation instead of just letting it remain unsaid.

As you build the habit of calling out misalignment, it will start to provoke new decisions, because you and your team leaders will start to feel the weight of being stuck. The intentional dialogue used to build your team commitments, along with the shared language you've developed, will make it easier to take on tough conversations and be honest about the trade-offs you are making.

Scenario Testing

One of my favorite parts of working with a team to define their *HOW* is when we do *scenario testing*. We identify scenarios they know for sure are going to come up, and we start to play around with how the team commitments they've articulated will be put into practice to change the outcomes.

Staying true to your *HOW* when inevitable scenarios arise can feel scary, uncomfortable, or downright dangerous. Staying aligned during turbulent times is tough to do. It means going back to the work of identifying mindsets and group dynamics that keep you stuck in old patterns and staying connected to the shifts that are required to create change. Luckily, practice helps, and talking through scenarios before they happen will help drive new outcomes in the moment.

A good scenario is something you can predict will happen based on past experiences, where you can compare how you and your team responded historically with how you intend to respond in the future. Consider these guidelines when coming up with scenarios to test your team commitments:

» Is this a situation you have seen play out in the past and believe will play out in the future?

» Is the situation or your organization's response to it directly influenced by how your team works or leads together?

» Is the situation easily understood by all members of the team?

» Does the situation require excessive detail or knowledge to test it against the team commitments? If so, you may want to bring it up a level.

» Can you see how you and your team would respond differently if you were truly bringing your team commitments to life?

What are the scenarios you and your leadership team should discuss? Here are a few to get the conversation moving:

SCENARIO 1

Quarterly numbers are due, and your sales team is coming up short because they are transitioning into new ways of selling.

SCENARIO 2

Budgets are being set, and you need additional resources to support a transformation effort happening in your area.

SCENARIO 3

You are asked by the board to provide an update on an important initiative, and you are very short on time to develop it.

SCENARIO 4

Your team is pushing back on adopting processes from another region because it is creating additional work for them.

What are the types of scenarios you and your team should talk about? If you've done the work throughout this book to identify your influencers, consider your new decisions and behaviors, and build *P-HOWS* to support them, you can consider scenarios that are specific to your team commitments. Don't hesitate to grab a piece of paper, write your list here, or download the When It Gets Hard worksheet.

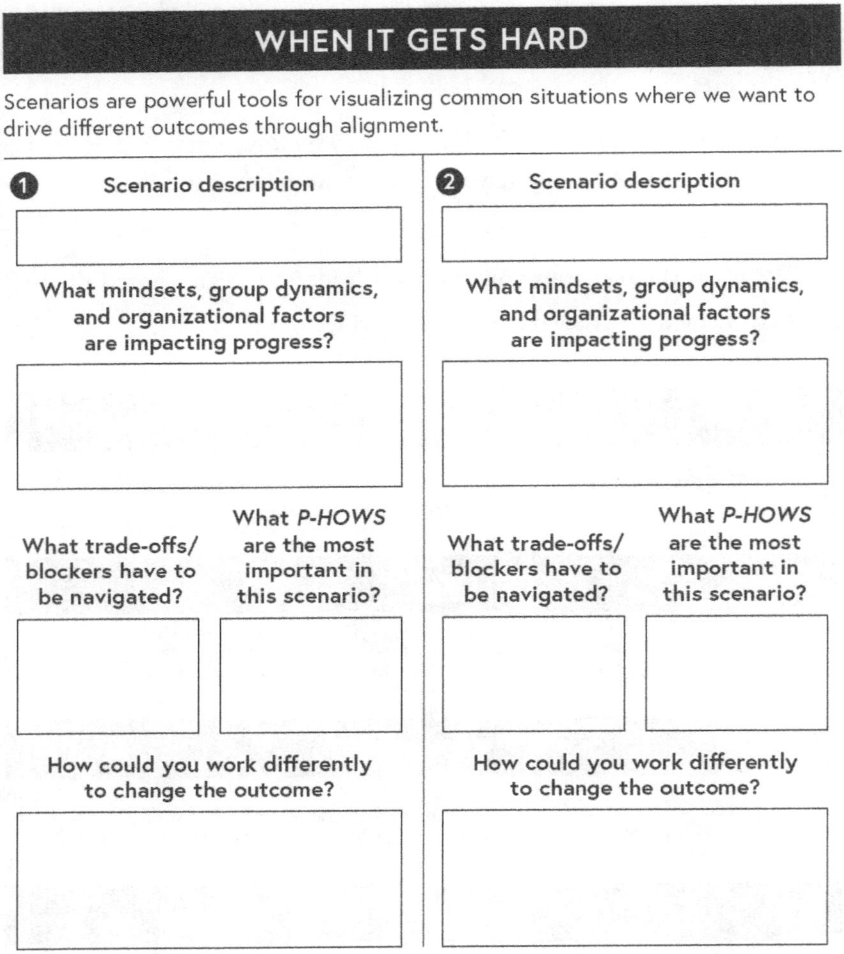

WHEN IT GETS HARD

Scenarios are powerful tools for visualizing common situations where we want to drive different outcomes through alignment.

1 Scenario description

2 Scenario description

What mindsets, group dynamics, and organizational factors are impacting progress?

What mindsets, group dynamics, and organizational factors are impacting progress?

What trade-offs/ blockers have to be navigated?

What *P-HOWS* are the most important in this scenario?

What trade-offs/ blockers have to be navigated?

What *P-HOWS* are the most important in this scenario?

How could you work differently to change the outcome?

How could you work differently to change the outcome?

Image 6.1: When It Gets Hard Worksheet

Scenarios will help you to navigate the moments when you know it will get hard to stay aligned to your new team commitments.

Let's take one last look at our two case studies, TT1 and SnackInvasion, to see what scenarios might be helpful for them.

Tech Team 1 Scenarios

Let's take a look at TT1 and SnackInvasion to better understand scenario testing for team commitments.

As a reminder, TT1 wanted more collaboration. They had three team commitments to drive this goal:

1. Check in first

2. Respect the invitation

3. Expansive, not embarrassing

As TT1 aligned to their team commitments, they could start testing scenarios where they knew it would be hard to do.

Scenario 1

The team got together with senior executives every quarter to present their QBRs. Historically, they prepared them independently with very little cross-over between what they were doing as team leaders. In the meetings, they sat silently as each person presented a detailed PowerPoint presentation to the executives. There was little to no collaborative discussion in the meetings.

New Approach

» Through their scenario work, they decided to try something new in their next QBR. Instead of creating fifty-page slide decks per region, they built one-page outlines of the key points for their areas of the business. Then they grouped areas together to explore connections and to highlight leverage points that they could discuss with senior leaders.

» They "checked in first" with one another and compared notes to see where there was duplication, opportunities for leverage, and places they could present together on key topics.

» For areas where one leader was the clear expert but others had ideas to contribute, they reminded one another to "respect the invitation" by being clear about who had a voice, a vote, and a veto over what was presented in that area.

Outcome

» By building the content outline together, they gained confidence their colleagues could engage in dialogue with the executives without putting anyone on the spot. By presenting some topics together, they were more comfortable opening up to questions and observations from the executives.

» By being better connected to one another, they reduced the amount of time spent preparing individual reports, and the number of slides in most areas was cut almost in half.

» The executive leaders began to see them as a cohesive and powerful unit rather than as individuals with limited perspectives and scopes.

» They had a lot more fun working together and came away with a better appreciation of the business as a whole. They discovered they could create more leverage across the team because they were making better decisions as a result of their deeper connections.

Scenario 2

It wasn't uncommon for a senior executive to reach out to a team member with an urgent request for data or a solution to a problem. Typically, the person who got the call immediately kicked into high gear, working the problem in isolation. They frequently found out later that several team members were working on the same problem without knowing it.

New Approach

» In order to "check in first," team members acknowledged their instinct to win by being the fastest to respond. That was hard for some of them, but with the shared language they had developed, they were able to express their concerns about being unresponsive. They needed a quick and reliable way to check in with one another on urgent executive requests while also getting started on addressing them. They decided to use a specific Slack channel called Executive Requests to share things. If they saw a message pop up in that channel, they'd review it and respond within twenty-four hours if they were working on the same issue or if they had ideas to contribute.

» One of the mindsets that had surfaced in their intentional dialogue about shifts was that some requests were particularly interesting to work on or provided a platform for exposure to the executive team. So, being more transparent about the requests required them to "respect the invitation" and not grab an opportunity or dominate a solution effort if it looked especially interesting.

» This created some difficult moments for the team, but because they had done the work to build their team commitment to *HOW* they wanted to work together, they were able to work through those moments in new ways.

Outcome

» By checking in on urgent executive requests, the team started to build a new rhythm for working together and managing upward.

» They created more capacity for themselves by reducing duplicate efforts across their teams.

» Executives stopped viewing them as individual leaders and started to engage with them as a cohesive team of leaders who could be a powerful force for change and transformation in the company.

CASE STUDY

SnackInvasion Scenario

Let's loop back with SnackInvasion and see how they could use scenarios to lean into their team commitments. As a reminder, Sandy and Jordon's team at SnackInvasion was struggling with transformation. They had four team commitments to drive the multiyear transformation they were undertaking:

1. Start with we aren't so different.

2. Remember that we all have our own journeys to the same destination.

3. Challenge ourselves first, then our people.

4. Have the conversation.

The SnackInvasion team identified a very common scenario where it would be hard to stick with the transformation as a priority, and where the pull of business as usual would be strong.

Scenario 1

Employee engagement was dropping because people were being asked to do too much to support the transformation and still meet aggressive sales and growth goals. In the past, regional presidents had responded by pulling their people out of transformation assignments or giving them permission to opt out of spending time on that work.

New Approach

» By having the conversation with one another about the workload in their areas and remembering that they *aren't so different*, they could leverage one another's ideas and resources to keep things moving forward while helping their employees stay engaged.

» If they *challenged themselves first*, they saw that they weren't doing what they needed to as leaders to push back on the historical expectations that were being imposed. By unifying their voices and speaking up as a leadership team, they had more power than any one of them speaking up individually and feeling like a squeaky wheel.

» By remembering that they were *all on their own journeys*, they were able to work together to adjust the pacing for regional needs while still moving toward the shared outcomes of the transformation.

Outcome

» These sometimes subtle shifts in the conversations leaders were having created big changes over time in the outcomes they delivered. By consistently coming back to their new commitments to transforming how they worked together, the leaders connected more frequently and more productively about big issues that they were all struggling with.

» Small changes done consistently over time create big new outcomes, and these nudges into new ways of leading together helped the team unify their voices as leaders to become powerful advocates for progress in the transformation while continuing to drive the business forward.

All of this takes consistent effort over time, but it doesn't take enormous effort every day. Like learning any skill, you don't get better by just doing it in a high-stakes moment; you get better by practicing and then applying your practice. You don't get better at playing Tchaikovsky's piano pieces by just sitting down and playing them beginning to end; you get better by doing endless repetitions of scales and exercises while running through small chunks until you've built the muscle memory. If you want to learn how to play tennis, you don't start by playing against world-class players; you start by hitting balls against a wall, and then over a net. And world champion sports teams don't spend all their time playing in games; they spend hours practicing together so they know how to win when it counts. Practice using your team commitments in small ways so when big moments come, you'll be ready. By staying aligned, you'll show up as a team and deliver new outcomes in amazing ways, even in very challenging scenarios.

The Courage to Act

I believe it takes individual and collective action to make different choices when it's easier to tread a well-worn path. But action takes courage, and *courage* is a tricky word. It is laden with cultural beliefs about superheroes and antiheroes, those who suffer and those who lead the charge into battle. And in many cultures, it is used to describe extraordinary individuals who are adventurous risk-takers, those who dare greatly or sacrifice much to advance society or save others. Those are lofty ideals of courage!

The thing is, in leadership, courage is required in thousands of small moments when people make unexpected decisions to try something a little different. It is occasionally about those big, heroic moments, but frequently it's about holding the line and staying true to the simple but powerful commitments you've made about *HOW* to lead together.

When it comes to *HOW* to lead together to create transformative outcomes for your organization, I think about the following five acts of courage needed to leap the Failure Gap:

1. To have hard conversations about topics people might rather avoid

2. To hold yourself and others accountable to doing your own hard work

3. To be a part of something bigger than yourself as a part of a leadership team

4. To invite others into your domain by allowing others to help you

5. To nudge yourself and others as you shift mindsets, group dynamics, and trade-offs while navigating organizational factors and blockers

When I work with teams, I first ask the leaders to start with themselves. How, as leaders, are they are showing up? Do individuals have what it takes to hold themselves to new standards, regardless of what others do? Then we move to the team. Does the team have the connective fiber to hold members accountable to behavioral standards and new decisions and to try new ways of working together, even if it means risking coming up short or failing? Courage comes in all shapes and sizes, and in this work, I am looking for the courage it takes to do something new, to have different conversations, to call attention to often-invisible pressures, to trust a colleague, to ask for help as well as giving it, to risk reputation, or to have hard conversations about accountability with colleagues, peers, and friends. It isn't running into a burning building, but it all takes courage nonetheless.

What about you and your leadership team? Do you and your colleagues have the courage to:

» Change the status quo in ways that put *fine* at risk

» Try something different

» Risk your reputation for reliably delivering results

» Allow others to shine by creating the space for them to contribute to your success

» Bring other people into your world

» Make trade-offs that benefit the enterprise instead of your piece of it

» Talk about the influencers that are driving team decisions and investments

How else will aligning take courage from you and your colleagues in your particular environment? Have a conversation with your colleagues about the situations where they feel like it gets hard to have the courage to work differently together. How can you all work together to create an environment where it is easier to stay accountable to new behaviors?

Dig Deep Through Dialogue

As you go forward, lots of "easy to say but hard to do" ideas will come up quickly, and being ready for them is the best way to make sure they don't disrupt progress. The reason I emphasize *intentional dialogue* as you work to create your *HOW* is because through dialogue, you connect and create a level of shared understanding that can spark courageous decisions and behaviors when things get hard, as they always do.

Image 2.6: Karrikins Alignment Competency Model

Remember, clarity and connection are used to define your *HOW*. Commitment brings *HOW* to life through new decisions and behaviors, and courage sustains it over time. That's why the last step in *making HOW matter* is to lean into the courage it takes to put your work into action and to stay focused as you go forward. Alignment ebbs and flows over time, and your outcomes will change as you achieve goals and move forward. But the muscle and strength you've built through the conversations in this book will help you to push for aligned action on any goal through intentional dialogue that clarifies and connects with the influencers, drives commitment, and fuels the courage to stay the course. It will help you keep moving forward together.

Have the courage to do small things consistently over time, and you will change the outcomes you and your colleagues deliver in ways you can't even imagine.

KEY TAKEAWAYS

- » You can support accountability to your team commitments by building routines for you and your colleagues.

- » Cascading your team commitments deeper into your organization can help you maintain alignment by creating more awareness and visibility about how you want to lead together.

- » Role clarity helps you build stronger alignment, because people won't have to guess about what's expected of them.

- » It is better to honestly say "This is misaligned, and we are doing it anyway" than to try to creatively make the decision sound aligned.

- » You will feel the incredible pull of the status quo as you work to shift into new ways of leading together. Resist this by continuing to have conversations about alignment.

- » Scenarios are a powerful way of flexing your team commitments and learning how to use them to take new actions in difficult moments.

Check out www.makehowmatter.com/worksheets
for more resources.

When someone says, "I agree," ask them, "How are we going to do this together?"

Go Make *HOW* Matter

The beginning is the most important part of the work.

—Plato, philosopher

YOU'VE MADE IT THIS FAR, so congratulations on your progress, and thank you for stepping into my world of *making HOW matter*!

You might be wondering what to do next. In fact, I hope you are. Throughout this book, you've had the opportunity to lean into new conversations with your colleagues to understand how you are impacting your teams and your business. Now it's time to put those into practice.

If you haven't already, take the work you've done throughout this book to your colleagues to get their input. Host conversations. Invite questions. What do they think is cool? What would they change? Build your Diamond Triangle as a team, taking the time to engage in intentional dialogue about *HOW* to lead differently together. You and your team will discover the mindsets, group dynamics, and organizational factors getting in the way of the outcomes you'd most like to see. These are powerful discussions, and you may want an outside facilitator to help support you, but you can start with the resources in this book and on our resources page: www.makehowmatter.com/worksheets.

Remember, you can't do this in isolation and then tell people the answers—you need to do it in connection with others on your team. It is in conversation that the team establishes enough shared meaning to take the outcomes forward together.

When you do the work to bring clarity and connection and build commitments together, you'll have the collective courage to behave differently as a team. You'll feel confident having intentional dialogue that results in transformational change. Pace yourselves and do this work steadily over time to allow a shared understanding to develop. When you take this approach, you will build the connections needed for team members to have the courage to change themselves and *HOW* they lead individually and collectively. When new ways of working are rushed or crammed into a catalytic event, like a one-day off-site seminar, the connections aren't strong enough to withstand difficult moments.

> **When you do the work to bring clarity and connection and build commitments together, you'll have the collective courage to behave differently as a team.**

If you only take one thing away from this book, I hope it is the importance of leaders starting with self and asking the question: How am I/are we going to lead differently to deliver on this? Before you try to change, transform, or otherwise move other people, think about how your own leadership needs to shift toward different outcomes. Remember, if you think you don't need to change how you lead, you are probably not transforming your organization.

When people see you starting with self, visibly learning, growing, and changing, you will create an unstoppable ripple effect in your company. The degree to which this one habit will energize your team can't be understated—you will be amazed at how generative it is and how much influence it has over your team. People are quickly bored or disenchanted by leaders who are unwilling to learn anything new. Be the leader who infuses energy and excitement into transformation by sharing your journey.

If you've gone through the conversations in this book, you now have a rich and diverse set of tools and resources for identifying misalignment and building ways of working together to align and activate transformation in your organization. Over time, you will build the habit of always asking the question: *HOW* are we going to do this together?

This work takes time, effort, and intention. You and your team have to do the work, just like you have to do your own training runs to finish a marathon. By following the structure and approach within these pages, you can make the process more productive, engaging, and fun. The Karrikins Diamond Triangle and the Karrikins Behavior Model, together with the Four *C*s of the Karrikins Alignment Competency Model and the worksheets in this book, are designed to facilitate the right discussions in the best possible approach to help you on your way.

The process of building your *HOW* is engaging and generative. When you are done with the first effort, those around you will have a built-in understanding of what it means. Done right, you and your colleagues will know how to spot agreement and push for alignment on your most important work together, giving you the energy and momentum to move through the Failure Gap and deliver new outcomes for your organization. It is a muscle the team can build over time through small shifts in how you discuss, debate, and decide what to do as you move forward.

From my desk to yours, I wish you all the best as you bring the power of alignment to your organization. I have confidence that you can and will reach success as you do this worthy and hard work of building clarity and connection, committing to new ways of working, and having the courage to *make HOW matter*.

Acknowledgments

FIRST, I WANT TO THANK my family and friends for all the care and understanding. I know I work in odd rhythms, and I couldn't ask for a better support system.

To all the Karrikins out there—the past, current, and future colleagues, clients, and friends of the firm—thank you for your support, engagement, and the leaps of faith people have taken to do the hard work and get aligned to shared goals.

Brent Bowman, Daniel Raffield, Nicole Winkler, and Kate Zappitelli: a huge thank-you to the four of you for showing up every day to do the work of helping people align and deliver together.

Peter Sheahan, thank you for including me in part of your adventure. I appreciate your support and your confidence in me.

Bruce Siegel, thank you for your support and unwavering belief in the work we do. Without your partnership, this book would not have been possible.

Our publisher, Greenleaf, has been invaluable in making this project a reality. I so appreciate the patience, support, and expertise they have provided.

And thank you to all the people who are doing this work—it is hard, it matters, it changes the outcomes you deliver, and it has an impact on the world. I believe in you.

About the Author

Julie Williamson, PhD
CEO and Managing Partner,
Karrikins Group

In an increasingly digitized world, leadership is becoming increasingly human. Julie's powerful combination of expertise in business, technology, and social science creates a unique perspective on solving the challenges that live in that reality. It is through the intersection of those skills that Julie helps leaders and their teams focus on the work that matters most for colleagues, customers, and communities.

Julie works with leaders around the world as they tackle some of the biggest challenges in their industries and organizations. In today's complex and interconnected world, Julie knows the power of aligned leaders to deliver on strategy and create value. That's why she focuses her time and energy on helping senior leaders come together. In addition to leading Karrikins Group, Julie is a keynote speaker, spreading the word about the importance of *making HOW matter* for leaders, especially during times of transformation and change.

For more about Julie's background, education, and publications, or to book her as a speaker, please visit her bio page at www.makehowmatter .com/julie.

www.ingramcontent.com/pod-product-compliance
Lightning Source LLC
Chambersburg PA
CBHW030515210326
41597CB00013B/915